MARX AND THE
ORTHODOX
ECONOMISTS

Other books by Pat Sloan

Soviet Democracy
Russia Without Illusions
How the Soviet State is Run
Russia Friend or Foe?
Russia in Peace and in War
Russia Resists
John Cornford—A Memoir (Edited by Pat Sloan)

MARX AND THE ORTHODOX ECONOMISTS

PAT SLOAN

'The average member of the capitalist class, when he discusses socialism, is condemned an ignoramus out of his own mouth . . .

'It is surely time that the capitalists knew something about this socialism that they feel menaces them.'

JACK LONDON

ROWMAN AND LITTLEFIELD
TOTOWA, NEW JERSEY

First published in the United States 1973
by Rowman and Littlefield, Totowa, N.J.

© Basil Blackwell 1973

LIBRARY OF CONGRESS CATALOGING IN PUBLICATION DATA

Sloan, Pat.
    Marx and the orthodox economists.

    1. Marxian economics. 2. Socialism.
3. Capitalism. I. Title.
HB97.5.S563   1973   335.4   73-5917
ISBN 0-87471-195-9

Printed in Great Britain

Contents

Preface

Having graduated in Economics at Cambridge, lectured for two years on the subject in Britain in a junior university post, and then having launched out on the 'adventure' of working in the USSR, where I stayed for five years, I ended up a Marxist.

In recent years I have again been teaching Economics in Britain, strictly within the syllabus, but for many years the idea has been maturing that a book was needed, today more than ever, to explain what Marx really did say and to show clearly the difference between the two approaches to Economics, of the 'orthodox' capitalist school on the one hand, and of the Marxists on the other.

As time has gone on I have become increasingly aware that both approaches may be labelled (whatever they may say about each other in polemics) as being scientific, so long as they accept as given a particular field of study. This book tries to outline the main differences between the two approaches, and ends with a consideration of the world's two dominant rival social systems of capitalism and socialism.

I am indebted first of all to Professor Joan Robinson of Cambridge for setting me on my way. In a letter, I casually mentioned such a book to her, at a time when nothing was down on paper at all. Her immediate response was to suggest the Publisher who has now accepted the book. I am also grateful to Mr D. J. Harris of Wisconsin, USA, recommended to me by Professor Robinson, and who has made many most useful comments on the manuscript.

Lifelong gratitude is also due to Maurice Dobb of Cambridge, for a number of reasons: For helping me, in his capacity of 'supervisor', to acquire my original grounding in 'orthodox' Economics. For periodically advising me, over more than forty years, on a variety of questions both of orthodox Economics and of Marxist Political Economy. And, finally, for reading the first draft of this book and, as always, giving useful professional advice.

I wish also to thank my old friend John Gibbons with whom I worked on Moscow Radio in the early 1930s and who has had many years of experience working in the international Communist movement, and who, like Maurice Dobb, has made useful suggestions. In his case, he emphasises, his comments have been entirely non-professional. But they have been useful.

Thanks are due to Librarians and their assistants; at the Marx Memorial Library, Clerkenwell, and at two branches of the Public Library of the London Borough of Bromley. All have been most helpful.

Needless to say, the final draft is all my own work and nobody else should be expected to share the blame.

Note

All page references to *Capital*, Vols. I, II, and III, are to the Kerr (Chicago) edition.

CHAPTER ONE

Introduction

When a person is solely dependent on earnings from work for a livelihood (unless 'self-employed') he is dependent on someone else for a job. His regularity or security of employment then depend on the interests and decisions of others over whom he, as 'employee', has no control. All who have at any time suffered from redundancy are aware of this from first-hand experience. All who have felt, at one time or another, that they were being paid less than they were worth, have also experienced a sense of being 'exploited'. And it is worth bearing in mind that in Britain today the majority of breadwinners are wage or salary-earners, working for somebody else, cogs in somebody else's machine over which they have no ownership or control. We have in Britain some 22 to 23 million 'employees', not to mention a million or so unemployed. As against all these, there are no more than 2 million employers and self-employed persons combined. This gives Britain an overwhelming majority of 'cogs'.

But when a person can live on what the Inland Revenue, with unconscious Marxism, describes as 'unearned income', whether it comes in the form of rents or interest, he is not dependent on employment for an income. He is 'independent'. And even if he works hard in a business of his own, he is still 'independent' in comparison with anyone whom he may see fit to employ.

There are thus, in our economic system, two major groups: the employers, the 'entrepreneurs' of orthodox economics, the 'capitalists' or 'bourgeoisie' of Marx. These range from shareholders and their directors to owner-managers. On the other hand are the subordinate salary and wage-earners, 'labour', Marx's 'proletariat'. In addition there are of course many intermediate strata, but forming only a relatively small minority. These are the 'self-employed', the freelance professionals who do not employ labour, and the small family businesses, mainly in retail trade, which are self-sufficient labour-wise. But nowadays, even in the professions, many employ labour and are in fact employers, while many more are employed full-time by particular organisations or firms, and never entirely free from the risk of possible redundancy due to rationalisation or the merger of enterprises. Even chairmen of nationalised industries are not immune nowadays from 'the sack'.

With such fundamentally different relations to production, it is natural that people should have different attitudes to what, in essence, are the same economic problems. This may seem to over-simplify, for plenty of individual examples may be found which are exceptions to this broad generalisation, but the generalisation itself nevertheless contains a volume of truth. So, too, while British economists have almost always seen everything from a distinctly British capitalist standpoint (except for a small maverick minority such as J. A. Hobson, G. D. H. Cole and a few other critics of capitalism and imperialism), economists born and bred in the colonies and former colonies, faced with the problems from their end, are likely to see things somewhat differently. There may be certain basic truths common to both, as, for example, that to consume it is necessary to produce (or at least to borrow, beg or steal). But fundamentally their approaches are likely to differ in many respects. In a particular situation, we should ask, are they on the side of lenders or borrowers, donors or beggars, employers or employed, or, in Marxist terminology, exploiters or exploited?

To those who live satisfactorily on income from dividends, there is no objective reason why they should contemplate the replacement of a system which works to their advantage; though some, if they find that the system has failed them, may begin to have doubts. Or again, if they have an exceptional social conscience—such as the three outstanding British businessmen socialists of the last century, Frederick Engels, William Morris and Robert Owen—then even they, despite their social and economic status, may arrive at the conclusion that the existing economic system, although it objectively provides them personally with profits, could be usefully replaced by one which more closely served the interests of the community as a whole.

As a result of the basic differences in class society, two schools of Political Economy emerged during the last century. On the one hand was the succession from the 'father' of English Political Economy, Adam Smith, *via* Marshall, to the orthodox Economics of the English-speaking world today. The term 'orthodox' is used throughout this book to distinguish the particular stream of economic thought known in the English-speaking world as 'Economics'.

The second stream of economic thought was that enunciated by Marx and Engels, who followed up critically certain lines indicated by Adam Smith and Ricardo. While the orthodox school took as given the private ownership of the means of production (land and capital), and lumped them together with labour, and more recently 'enterprise', as 'factors of production'; it saw them all as receiving a 'reward' or 'return' for their use in production, and treated them all as more or less equal bargainers in ascertaining the rate of return paid.

The Marxists, on the other hand, regarded the economic system historically, in terms of constantly changing social relations, in which, at the present stage, the basic conflict lies in the antagonistic interests of owners and workers. Although many subsequent Marxist writings have come from those who were primarily 'politicians', this does not in any way negate the value of their work as economists. Lenin, Bukharin, Rosa Luxemburg, and many others may be mentioned, all of whom tend to be ruled out from respectable consideration because of their 'politics'.

For nearly a century Marx and Marxism have been almost taboo to orthodox economists. The dismissal of Marx from serious study has taken the form of his exclusion from economics syllabuses, on the spurious ground that his work was 'political' *and/or* not scientific. Yet, on the Marxist side, it is claimed that the study of capitalism on the basis of Marx's work is an essential ingredient of 'scientific socialism'.

On perusing the present book, readers may well ask, 'are all the original quotations from Marx really necessary?' Nowadays we do not quote extensively from Adam Smith, Ricardo, John Stuart Mill and the rest, so why, in the case of Marx, should we behave differently?

Now if Marx had received 'normal' treatment at the hands of orthodox economists (I am not suggesting that this was possible in the social context of capitalism), his work would have been incorporated into their 'folk memory' as, indeed, has happened with the classical economists of capitalism. In that case, there would have been no need to quote him so much today in order to recall what he really did say, in face of the many distortions to which he has been subjected.

Although Marx devoted voluminous writings to a critique of his contemporaries and predecessors—Adam Smith, Ricardo, John Stuart Mill and James Mill, McCulloch, Sir William Petty and others from Britain; Blanqui, Proudhon, Quesnay and Say from France; Rodbertus and Sismondi from Germany and Switzerland, and a score more; his voluminous work on this has never been recognised by the orthodox, and has only finally been edited by the Marx-Lenin Institute in Moscow and published under the title of *Theories of Surplus Value* (Vol. IV of *Capital*). While collecting material for this work, Marx once wrote to Engels that the project was for a 'historico-literary' book. He wrote these words in 1865, just before Vol. I of *Capital* appeared in German. Though Marx and Engels did not live long enough to see the publication of 'Vol. IV', and the Marx-Lenin Institute had to finish the job, it now exists in the English language. Nobody, however 'orthodox', could read this volume today and deny that Marx was a great economist however unpalatable his 'political', i.e. working-class, approach to the subject might be.

Surveying the ground, then, it is not unreasonable, even at this apparently late stage, to quote so many of the original formulations provided by Marx himself. A time will no doubt come when the Political Economy of Socialism will be so mature that its contemporary writers, having absorbed the groundwork bequeathed by Marx, will be exploring new problems with only rare references to the 'founding fathers'. In the Socialist countries this is already happening, and we can only hope that if ever Marxist Political Economy becomes dominant in the world, it may be more charitable to the orthodox economists of capitalism than the orthodox have been towards the Marxists.

The pressure of world events since 1945 has already had some effect in the West. The successes of the USSR in the Second World War (despite all predictions to the contrary), the increase in the number of governments accepting Marxist Political Economy, the tendency for many newly independent countries to lean towards some form of economic planning, of which the USSR is the world's first example, and the increase in the public sector even in such capitalist countries as Britain—have all contributed to this development.

But even today the number of Western economists who may be said to have taken Marx seriously is pitifully small. Maurice Dobb, now retired from his lectureship at Cambridge, is one example. Professor Joan Robinson, also of Cambridge, is another. Among the younger lecturers in British universities there are now a few more. But comparatively few. In the United States such economists as P. A. Baran and P. M. Sweezy have done outstanding work in Marxist economics; and one deviator from the orthodox tradition, J. A. Schumpeter, produced a theory of the origins of economic crisis which bore a striking resemblance to Marx's approach. Needless to say, the orthodox have tended to ignore him. On the other hand, J. M. Keynes, whose analysis of crises bore much more similarity to that of Marx than Keynes himself ever acknowledged, has won worldwide acceptance for his contribution to a 'revolution' within orthodox economics itself.

A common pitfall in dealing with Marx is to forget that (a) his total work extended over a period of more than forty years, and his major work, CAPITAL, was never completed during his lifetime. He therefore had no opportunity to go over the whole completed work, eliminating inconsistencies and repetitions, and clarifying ambiguities. (b) Marx's work is conducted at different levels of abstraction according to its context, and a generalisation which is appropriate at one level—such as what people have christened the 'law' of 'increasing misery' (see Chap. 7) or 'law' of the 'declining rate of profit' (see Chap. 4)—may be quite inappropriate when we are discussing the actual ways in which these *tendencies*, for they are no more than this, are offset in real life by counter-tendencies which Marx himself underlined.

Finally, (c), conditions themselves change. Competition, as forecast by Marx, has led to even larger units and so to monopoly; and this demands a certain amount of re-thinking concerning the relationship of the Labour Theory of Value to prices.

In the West, Economics has tended to develop along its own lines, obsessed with the prevalent problems of capitalism. In the 1920s and 1930s the focus of attention was on unemployment; in the 1950s and 1960s it has been on inflation and the Balance of Payments. In the 1970s, again, unemployment comes to the fore. However, the growth of public ownership in a number of non-socialist countries has forced itself upon the attention of economists so that nowadays, unlike the 1930s, the 'public sector' is accepted as something normal, while before 1939 it was still treated by most orthodox economists as a fringe abnormality in a 'private enterprise' system.

The Political Economy of Marx has remained the basis for developments in the 'Communist' or 'Planned Economy' countries, because it was Marx and his followers who, as an alternative to capitalism, posed public ownership of the means of production and the planning of their utilisation and expansion in the interests of society. In this case, however, because of the inevitable link between economic doctrine and political polemic; and of the need for greater unanimity among theoreticians when their collective views have to be incorporated in state policy; there has economy with regard to estimates of wants and resources, production and co-ordination.

In the present book it is not possible to do more than scratch the surface of the fascinating study of where the paths of the two separate schools of thought have crossed. At this stage we are only concerned with underlining the main differences, which cannot be understood unless based on a knowledge of what Marx really did say. It is hoped that readers, by the end, will at least appreciate that it is quite wrong, and unscientific, to dismiss Marx and Marxism as worth less attention than the traditional school of orthodox Economics.

been less flexibility in the development of Marxist Political Economy in the face of changing circumstances than might have been desirable. There have been tendencies to dogmatism in adhering to particular formulations of Marx while ignoring his own quite comprehensive escape clauses; and in the USSR, during the last years of Stalin, there was an internal dogmatism such that nobody apart from Stalin dared to voice a new idea, even on the basis of Marx's own original exploratory work. Since the death of Stalin this unfortunate cause of frustration has been removed, and now economists in the USSR are once more able freely to disagree with one another within the basic school of Marxist Political Economy and its application to the modern world.

In both Britain and the USA today students are considerably insulated against the impact of Marxism. In the case of Britain, both economics textbooks and examination syllabuses are orientated on the 'gospels' according to Marshall, Keynes and the post-Keynsians. Equally, in the socialist countries, textbooks and syllabuses are based on the 'gospels' of Marx, Engels and Lenin. Neither side, at least at student level, is encouraged to probe into the standpoint of the other. It may in fact be impracticable to do so in the time available. But that is another matter.

The present book is an attempt to highlight in a simple way, at the risk of oversimplification, the main differences between the approach of Marx and the approach of orthodox Economists; taking certain specific problems for the purpose of illustration.

First of all, as we must, we deal with the vexed question of scientific 'objectivity', for on this question each side accuses the other of being non-scientific. As we shall see, there is good ground for regarding each as being scientific *within its own terms of reference*.

We then proceed to discuss the 'Labour Theory of Value' of Marx and contrast it with the orthodox 'Theory of Value' which has, since Alfred Marshall, become entirely a 'theory of prices'.

From this it is a logical next step to consider the nature of profit; whether seen as the 'surplus value' of Marx or the 'return' for enterprise and risk-taking as it is seen in orthodox economics.

We next consider the two approaches to the subject of competition and monopoly. The difference here is fundamental, for while orthodox economics still leans towards approaching its 'free enterprise system' on the assumption that competition is the norm and monopoly some abnormal excrescence, Marx stressed from the first that—although his own analysis in depth assumed competitive conditions—monopoly was always the logical outcome to which successful competition would lead. To Marx the progress towards monopoly was the inevitable result of the growth in scale of the successful firms, and this was so at a time when all orthodox economists treated competitive capitalism as inviolable except in rare cases. To them, monopoly was a sort of illegitimate offspring, but to Marx it was an inevitable end-product.

We next come to one of the most controversial fields of discussion both in orthodox and in Marxist economics. This is the subject of what has variously been termed the 'trade cycle', 'business cycle', 'industrial fluctuations', and which, in Marxist terminology, is treated as but a symptom of what is described as the 'general crisis of capitalism'. Slumps, booms, unemployment and their causes have been discussed throughout the history of both Political Economy and Economics, and more than any other aspect this has been a subject of constant controversy within both schools.

The subject of planning, while touched upon by Marx, was only fully brought to life by the Marxists in power in the USSR from 1928 onwards. Nevertheless, contrasts between 'planned economies' and the 'free world' are repeatedly being made.

Linked to the above is the question of growth and development which naturally was paramount in the launching of the USSR's First Five Year Plan in 1928 and has remained a priority in all economic planning ever since. But in the West there was practically no serious discussion among economists of problems of growth, development and planning before 1945.

Finally, we are faced with two sectors of the world, in one of which there are socialist planned economies and the acceptance of

Marxist Political Economy, and in the other of which the 'free enterprise system' is still basic even though the public sector has grown considerably in a number of countries in the past twenty-five years. We now find advocates of the view that the two systems are 'converging', opposed by the alternative view that they can 'coexist' but that fundamental differences are too great for convergence to take place. And, of course, between the two basic systems, there is a 'third world' of countries whose future course of development is still unclear.

But whether or not the two systems are 'converging', they are at least trading increasingly with one another, despite sharp differences of view as to the political expediency of such trade. On both sides, whether through the organs of the United Nations, or the European Common Market, or COMECON, there are international agreements on trade and co-operation between countries which form part of the two basically different economic systems. There are also certain developments which proceed in parallel in the two systems, so that the West has its World Bank and the IMF while the countries of a planned economy have now set up their own International Investment Bank.

We therefore end this book on the note that increasing trade and co-operation is taking place between the two systems, where this is agreed to be to their mutual advantage, but that the theoretical differences between 'orthodox' Economics and Marxist Political Economy remain; just as the real differences remain between the private ownership of the means of production, and the public ownership and planned utilisation of them under Socialism.

The fundamental contrast is between the countries where in the main production is carried out for private profit, and the countries in which land and capital are now public property, utilised according to a general plan aimed both at raising living standards and continuous economic growth of the system. In brief, the contrast may be said to be between production for private profit and production for the welfare of the community; between 'free enterprise' or 'planning'. In drawing such a

B

contrast, however, we do not wish to suggest that, even under the former system, social welfare does not receive consideration. Especially since 1946 in Britain, it does. But this is still not the main motivation of the system.

Having stressed the fundamental distinction *between* the two 'camps' as they are sometimes called; we should now note the extent to which differences exist *within* each. The economic system of the United States differs in many respects from that of Britain, in spite of the growing volume of cross-investment which is taking place. Other countries, France, West Germany and Japan, Italy and Spain, Denmark and Portugal, New Zealand and Brazil, all have their specific characteristics, whether they are within the European Common Market or outside it. And, contrary to the misconceptions of many, there are also differences between the countries of the socialist world: The sharp political differences between the USSR and China have received much publicity, but their *economic* differences, though both claim to be applying Marxist methods to their own countries, are no less important. But even Poland and Bulgaria, Hungary and Czechoslovakia, the German Democratic Republic and Rumania all have their specifically national and historical features.

Despite these differences, the common features centred on the private ownership of the means of production, and production for private profit; and public ownership of the means of production and planned production for welfare and economic growth; remain fundamental. This is so even where a 'public sector' has bitten as far into the formerly private sector of such a 'free enterprise' country as Britain.

In considering either side in this great divide, it should never be forgotten that human beings and their institutions are not infallible. In both systems errors occur. But whereas it has been customary in orthodox economics to write off the errors of capitalism as merely 'adjustments' in the market, the errors of the planned economies have been paid exaggerated attention. Just as errors of business forecasting are fundamental to capitalism, so errors will continue to occur for a long time even under a planned economy with regard to estimates of wants and resources, production and co-ordination.

In the present book it is not possible to do more than scratch the surface of the fascinating study of where the paths of the two separate schools of thought have crossed. At this stage we are only concerned with underlining the main differences, which cannot be understood unless based on a knowledge of what Marx really did say. It is hoped that readers, by the end, will at least appreciate that it is quite wrong, and unscientific, to dismiss Marx and Marxism as worth less attention than the traditional school of orthodox Economics.

CHAPTER TWO

Objectivity, History and Class

In a book on *Elementary Economics* by J. Harvey, recommended to students by such professional bodies in Britain as the Institute of Bankers, an early distinction is drawn between 'Collectivism' and 'Capitalism'. Under the first term 'we can include Communism, Socialism and a Controlled Economy' while the latter comprises '*laissez-faire*, Private Enterprise, and an Uncontrolled Economy'. (Harvey, op. cit., p. 12.) The writer then proceeds to contrast the two systems as follows:

Collectivism: 'Here we may mention four criticisms of the system . . . the difficulties in estimating the size of all the various wants of a population . . . Secondly, many officials are required to estimate wants and to direct factors of production . . . Thirdly, . . . there are difficulties of co-ordination . . . Fourthly, it is argued that State ownership of the factors of production, by lessening incentives, diminishes effort and initiative'. (Ibid., pp. 12–13.)

When we come to capitalism we read that here 'emphasis is laid on the freedom of the individual, both as a consumer and as the owner of a factor or factors of production.

'As a consumer he expresses his wants through the price system' so that this 'price system is an integral part of an economy based on capitalism'. However, defects are enumerated to include 'great inequalities of wealth . . . disadvantages follow because profit is the dominant motive in production . . . if left entirely to private enterprise, some goods and services would not be produced . . . Fourthly, certain forms of competition themselves lead to waste . . . Fifthly, in practice, the competition . . . is liable to break down . . . Sixthly . . . the motive of private profit does not ensure that public wealth . . . will be maximised' and, 'most important of all, under Capitalism . . . there occur periods when factors of production are allowed to stand idle'. (Ibid., pp. 14–17.)

The reader is then told that the advantages of Capitalism 'correspond very closely to the defects of the Collectivist system'. For example, 'wants are easily gauged and changes in wants are reflected by changes in prices, other things being equal'. No mention is made of the losses incurred during adjustment under such a price system, nor is it mentioned that prices are also used in collectivist economies, and no reason is given for characterising the statistical estimation of wants on a national basis as 'difficult'. Secondly, the reader is informed that under capitalism 'owners . . . take . . . the factors of production . . . to where profit is highest', and this is assumed, without discussion, to be superior to a system aiming at rational allocation, presumably because the latter would involve 'many officials'. Nothing is said, incidentally, of a capitalist advantage to counterpose to the alleged collectivist disadvantage of 'difficulties of co-ordination'. Presumably because capitalist difficulties of co-ordination are greater, not less.

Capitalism, the reader is told, works 'without hosts of officials' while efficiency 'is achieved simply by using the incentive of private profit'.

But this balance sheet apparently is not enough, for finally there is added 'one big disadvantage of collectivism . . . the risk of being ruled by a dictator'. (Ibid., pp. 17–18.) This last excursion into naked politics might have been pardonable if, for the sake of objectivity, a list had been appended ranging from Hitler, to Voerster and the other dictators which the capitalist system has thrown up.

Moreover, while advantages are listed for capitalism, none are listed for collectivism. No mention is made of the positive results of economic planning, both in raising living standards and in providing for economic growth at a rapid rate, its increase in social services, and its protection of workers by means of legal minima of leisure, holidays, equal pay for equal work, and security of employment. While Harvey lists advantages of capitalism to balance against the disadvantages of socialism; he has forgotten to list the advantages of socialism which, to a great extent, replace his listed disadvantages of capitalism.

It remains a mystery why wants should be 'easily gauged' in a market economy, yet this should be 'difficult' as a result of a nation-wide study of demand trends and productive potentialities. And the writer fails to refer to the very distorted picture of 'wants' reflected by the market when incomes, as he admits, are subject to 'great inequalities'.

Again, to counterpose the 'many officials' under collectivism against an alleged lack of them under capitalism is totally unreasonable unless it allows for the 'many officials' of all the joint stock companies which conduct the business of the capitalist world. An official of ICI, Unilever or Barclays Bank is as much an official as the corresponding employee under a socialist economic Ministry. Moreover, to 'direct factors of production' according to estimated social usefulness is surely not less economically useful than to direct them according to estimated profit, especially when this system is so inefficient that it allows many resources 'to stand idle'.

As to 'incentives', 'it is said that State ownership' lessens them. (As to who says this, Harvey is mysteriously silent). But if we look, for example, at the USSR, we find that at all levels in the economy personal earnings are geared to the 'quantity and quality of their work', and this even includes awards for inventions and innovations in production of a kind which, in most capitalist enterprises, are appropriated *gratis* by employers.

Let us now turn to J. L. Hanson's widely used *Textbook of Economics* which has gone through four or five editions since it first appeared in 1953. Here we find the following crude comparison: 'In a free economy the consumer himself makes the choice; in the planned economy the choice rests with the State, acting through its planning committee'. (Hanson, op. cit., p. 9.) Not a word is said here about the fact that capitalist producers are themselves increasingly deciding what to produce and then, by means of advertising, indoctrinating consumers to 'want' what they have decided to produce. Not a word is said of the fact that in the countries with planned economies consumers also spend their earnings as they wish, are free from all but strictly informative advertising, and at all levels in the productive system they— as workers—play a part in discussing and drawing up the plans. Planning committees at all levels are concerned with the best utilisation of resources for satisfying the wants of the community as consumers and the long-term needs of economic growth.

These two examples, selected from current economics textbooks, are illustrations of the way in which, so soon as capitalist and socialist systems are compared, even conscientious orthodox economists slip into political prejudice and gross misstatement. Yet objectivity is surely an essential in any science.

When we turn to yet another popular textbook, Cairncross's *Introduction to Economics* we find that the subjective approach of economists is touched upon, albeit cautiously. For here we read that 'economics is of value in allowing us to judge and frame policies in the light of full knowledge of how the economic system works. Everyone, willy-nilly, is an economist, for everyone has his view of how economic forces work, and what, if anything, should be done to control them'.

In this sentence we have 'full knowledge', a bit optimistic, and everyone's 'own view'. But in reality economists disagree profoundly even when they claim the same 'full knowledge'. Cairncross puts this down to the existence of situations in which 'they do not share the same conception of social justice, or the same intuition of what is practicable. The more the problem admits of scientific treatment, the more do economists approach to unanimity'. (Cairncross, op. cit., p. 16.)

True, possibly, within the realm of orthodoxy, but even then a rather comforting doctrine. Cairncross, who shows more than usual sensitivity to the fact that economists disagree, still does not face up to the sort of difference which is based on the ownership, or non-ownership, of property. However, as we show later

(p. 105), he does go further than many in recognising the underlying importance of property ownership in capitalist society.

Let us now consider two more books which have recently been popular among students of orthodox economics. Their treatment of Marxism could hardly have been more different, yet each, in its way, contributes to the orthodox volume of ignorance of the subject. These books are Lipsey's *Introduction to Positive Economics* (2nd edn, 1966) and Samuelson's *Economics* (8th edn, 1970).

Lipsey treats Marxism, Socialism, Collectivism and the USSR as if they never existed, and does not mention them in his index. This sort of dismissal is hardly consistent with an objective study of existing economic systems, but it can of course be justified if it is accepted that Economics is exclusively the study of the economics of capitalism.

Samuelson, on the other hand, is superficially one of the most Marx-conscious of contemporary orthodox economists, but this does not prevent him from perpetuating myths about what Marx really said. It is true that, at one point, he dons the guise of objectivity by writing: 'A fair-minded reader of 1970—whether in Moscow, Idaho, or Moscow, Russia—will then' (after the perusal of later chapters) 'be in a position to judge whether the "labour theory of value" is of more than historical interest in the twentieth and twenty-first centuries'. (Samuelson, op. cit., p. 27.)

Unfortunately, those later chapters contain misleading references to Marx, as for example the statement that Marx's 'law of the declining rate of profit (or interest rate)' and 'law of the immiseration of the working class (falling real wage rate)' were both incorrect (Ibid., p. 725), and also, the latter idea is again expressed in the words that one of Marx's 'most famous' predictions, that 'the rich will become richer and the poor will become poorer . . . has proved to be quite wrong'. (Ibid., p. 106.)

Now in Chapter 7 we go fully into this 'most famous' prediction of Marx, and show that far from being an unqualified 'prediction' Marx did in fact also 'predict' a rising standard of life for the workers as a result of technological progress. The accident that one side of the picture became 'most famous' was due to both Marx's adulators and his denigrators, both of which groups, for their own purposes, stressed this one tendency in Marx's statements while keeping quiet about the opposing tendencies to which he also drew attention. Marx himself could hardly be blamed for this, except for the fact that, in each separate reference, he did not always couple with them the countervailing tendencies of which he was fully aware and to which he did draw attention in other passages.

As regards the 'falling rate of profit', Marx never at any time, as suggested by Samuelson, identified 'profit' in this context with 'interest'. It is too easy to try to discredit Marx by wrongly presenting what he wrote. (See Chapter 4.)

It may be felt by some readers that the above quotations from textbooks in general use, rather than from *magna opera* of the lions of the orthodox school, are cited because suitable material is lacking in those higher quarters. But this is not so. The only point of making so much of the textbooks is that it is that they are being mass-fed today to a whole generation of students of Economics.

To ascend Olympus for a single example, the following sneer at Marx by Keynes is worth recording: His theories, says Keynes, were 'illogical, obsolete, scientifically erroneous, and without interest or application to the modern world'. (Keynes, *Laissez-faire and Communism*, New York, 1926, p. 48, quoted in P. Mattick, *Marx and Keynes*, p. 21.) If this is the view of the pundit, why should even an advanced and sophisticated student of Economics waste his time on Marx?

No rule or generalisation is ever totally without some exception, and since work on this book was already in progress my attention was drawn by an Australian to one textbook which (though still unfair to Marx) stresses at the outset the need to study socialist planned economy as well as capitalism. This book is American, and represents quite a break from orthodox textbook tradition.

Economics—A General Introduction is by Professor Lloyd

Reynolds of Yale, and was first published in 1963. It opens with a significant message to teachers of economics who are told what, in essentials, has been maintained here. 'The standard allotment of space to the Soviet-bloc countries and the underdeveloped countries combined is about 5 per cent. This leaves the student ignorant of many matters in which he should be informed. It also breeds an ethnocentrism which regards his own economic institutions as right and proper, while all other nations are wrong-headed. The 20 per cent of space that I have allotted to foreign economics is still not enough, but is a step in the right direction.' (Op. cit., p. xi.)

It is still possible for the British student of a recommended book to find Planned Economy not considered at all. But in Professor Reynolds' book the existence of the two basically different economic systems is repeatedly recognised, and in this respect the author has achieved an important innovation.

However, he still succumbs to the orthodox malady of denigrating Marx, who is not even mentioned in his index, yet he cannot resist a sarcastic comment in relation to the USSR: 'There is also the ideological need to avoid any obvious imitation of capitalist methods and to sanctify any new departures by copious quotations from Marx. Fortunately, Marx wrote several thousand pages, many of them reasonably obscure, and this simplifies the task'. (Ibid., p. 66.)

It is unfortunate that while Professor Reynolds says a great deal more than any other writer of 'orthodox' textbooks on the subject of planned economies, his cursory dismissal of Marx and his systematic ignoring of the basic difference between *public* and *private* ownership of the means of production still perpetuate some of the orthodox weaknesses in dealing with the subject.

The above somewhat facetious reference to the USSR's 'ideological need to avoid any obvious imitation of capitalist methods' is definitely inaccurate (though possibly had some justification during the late Stalin period only). It was in 1918 that Lenin, in his pamphlet *On the Food Tax*, wrote that 'we must not be afraid to admit that . . . *we can and must learn a great deal from the capitalist'*. The USSR has demonstrated this in adapting the American 'Taylor system' of scientific management to Soviet conditions; in granting concessions to major capitalist companies to operate on Soviet soil; in employing the skills of capitalist engineers in building automobile works, the first line of the Moscow Metro, the Dnieper Dam and so on, right up to the agreement with Fiat to build the Togliatti motor works and the still more recent projects now under discussion with the USA. In all, Soviet history abounds in examples of 'learning from capitalism', and scientific, technological and cultural exchanges, to mutual advantage, are being negotiated with a growing number of capitalist countries. Light-minded treatment of such facts can only detract from the value of the new ground which Professor Reynolds has undoubtedly pioneered in orthodox economics teaching.

The orthodox economists of capitalism, despite a very considerable range of views, work on the basis of certain primary assumptions. These are the private ownership of the means of production, land and capital; that the suppliers of each 'factor of production' (land, capital, labour and enterprise) all receive a 'return' for their contribution to production determined by the interaction of Supply and Demand; and that the motive force in the system is the entrepreneur's striving for profit. On these assumptions a a major role is played by the interaction of Supply, Demand and Price. It is this system which goes by various names, including 'capitalist', 'free enterprise' or the 'market economy'.

The other approach, the Marxist one, views the development of property relations historically, and studies the 'laws of motion' by which they develop. Thus both landlordism and capitalism are seen as the result of a process of social and economic evolution from a time when land was communal and profit, as such, was unknown. It is this process which is studied.

From such a standpoint there is nothing permanent about capitalism. And as a result of studying its mechanics within the context of its development, Marx was able to point to certain 'contradictions' or conflicting tendencies within it by means of which, in due course, the system 'digs its own grave'. There is then likely to follow, as a result of these innate contradictions coupled with the political struggle and strengthening of the working class, the replacement of capitalism by socialism (a word now generally accepted to denote the 'first phase' of Marx's 'communism')—a system based on the public ownership of the means of production, the abolition in the main of 'unearned incomes', the replacement of the private profit motive by public planning for the betterment of the community, together with development, growth and rising living standards. As the end-product of such an evolution along new lines we come to a 'classless society', totally replacing the class-divided societies of the past.

Because Economics takes as its major premise the *status quo* in property relations; we find that the so-called 'free' economy is not only based on these relations, but that orthodox economics is limited in its scope to the discussion of problems arising *within* such a system. Controversies may rage fiercely on the alleged merits of Free Trade or Protection, Inflation or Devaluation, Prices and Incomes policies, or the prospects opened up by entering the European Common Market. But once an economist dares to overstep the mark and to question the economic usefulness of the private ownership of land and capital as such he is at once labelled a heretic, a socialist, communist or Marxist, and his 'economics' to the 'orthodox' becomes 'politics' and therefore suspect.

Because the Marxist starting point is, as Marx wrote in a different context, 'not to interpret the world differently, but to change it' (*Theses on Feuerbach*), its approach is that of an applied science combining research and analysis with their application in order to get results. The doctor who prescribes a course of treatment is being scientific (we hope), his aim is to cure the patient, but he is simultaneously studying the effects of the treatment and may modify it in the light of experience. Marxist economic analysis, comprehending society as a developing and changing phenomenon, with capitalism as but one stage in a long historical process, does not take existing property relations as sacrosanct but analyses their emergence, the conflicts to which they give rise, and prescribes for society the changes necessary to eliminate these sickly symptoms.

The capitalist system, regarded from the standpoint of all those who live on earnings from work, could be replaced by a system in which nobody any longer lived on 'unearned income'. This would provide society with the economic benefit of reducing the proportion of drones in the social hive, thus increasing the ratio of producers to consumers. It is thus in the interest of those who live on income from work to understand the dynamics of the rise and possible supersession of the capitalist system by one which is socially more beneficial. Therefore, in studying the development of economic systems historically, Marx included all pre-capitalist stages in his purview (in so far as they were, in his day, known). In one of his early works, *The German Ideology*, he already distinguished 'the first form of ownership as 'tribal', reaching its 'highest stage' in agriculture. Out of the 'natural division of labour imposed by the family' were evolved 'patriarchal chieftains; below them members of the tribe; finally slaves. The slavery latent in the family only develops gradually with the increase of population, the growth of wants, and with the extension of external relations, of war or of trade'. Hence evolved slavery, and also 'the antagonism between town and countryside; later the antagonism between those states which represent urban interests and those which represent country, and inside the towns themselves the antagonism between industry and maritime commerce'. Then develops a 'third form of ownership . . . feudal or estate property,' not now in slaves but 'landed property with serf-labour chained to it'. And in the towns there arises 'individual labour with small capital commanding the labour of journeymen'. At this stage, incidentally, usury was forbidden to Christians. ⅄

Then comes capitalism, first through the accumulation of merchant capital, and then in the development of industry. And so, in the *Communist Manifesto* of 1847 we find Marx's famous phrase that 'the history of all hitherto existing society is the history of class struggles'. (A footnote nowadays points to the fact that at that time researches into 'pre-history' were hardly known.) 'Freemen and slave, patrician and plebeian, lord and serf, guild-master and journeyman, in a word, oppressor and oppressed stood in constant opposition to one another.' Thence to today, the basic division of society into 'bourgeoisie and proletariat'.

It is under this system that production, instead of being carried out for the direct satisfaction of needs, is carried out to 'make money'. Goods are produced *for sale* instead of for direct use, and this system is characterised by Marx as 'commodity production'.

Marx's Political Economy is therefore historical in its basic approach, studying the *movement* of history. Orthodox economists limit themselves by their acceptance of the private ownership of the means of production, and production for profit, while the historical background is excluded, being relegated to the separate study of Economic History.

From Marx's standpoint pre-capitalist modes as well as the capitalist mode of production are all relevant parts of the study of man's eternal struggle to transform nature to serve his interests by creating 'use-values' which are 'combinations of two elements —matter and labour'. Man 'can work only as Nature does, that is by changing the form of matter'. So that, in essence, 'productive activity . . . is nothing but the expenditure of human labour-power'. (*Capital*, Vol. I, pp. 50–1.)

Seen in this light, economic activity is not something confined to the capitalist epoch, when land and capital are privately owned and 'commodities' are produced primarily for sale for private profit. This can be seen, in a historical setting, as simply one stage in mankind's economic evolution.

Marx did not denigrate the positive achievements of this stage, as is shown by the following passage: 'Modern industry has established the world market, for which the discovery of America paved the way. This market has given an immense development to commerce, to navigation, to communication by land. The development has in turn reacted on the extension of industry;

and in proportion as industry, commerce, navigation, railways extended, in the same proportion the bourgeoisie developed, increased its capital, and pushed into the background every class handed down from the Middle Ages'.

Thus capitalism 'is itself the product of a long course of development, of a series of revolutions in the modes of production and exchange'. (*Communist Manifesto*, Part I.)

With this broad historical approach Marxists see capitalism dynamically, in terms of how it arose, the 'contradictions' or antagonisms which pile up within the system as time goes on, and the only rational solution to these contradictions in a new mode of production, which may variously be called 'Communism', 'Socialism' or 'Collectivism'. The same system of production for private profit was originally a stimulus to progress so long as it was competitive. This was in spite of its inhuman exploitation of the men, women and children who had to work for wages, and the fact that it had ever more monopolistic features which have increasingly become a fetter on production. Thus, even if a monopolistic capitalism continues in being for a long time, its development of the productive forces remains strictly limited as compared to what could be achieved given social ownership and planning in the place of anarchy.

Economics in the West limits itself to this capitalist stage. While, on the one hand, it is argued that each factor of production receives a 'return', a price determined by Supply and Demand, so that all are equal participants in the supplying of their respective factors; on the other hand it is recognised that the supplier of enterprise, the entrepreneur, in return for anticipated profit, co-ordinates the use of the other three. According to Harvey, all the factors of production are supplied by 'free . . . owners, each of whom so conducts his affairs that he obtains as large a profit as possible . . . For many persons, the workers, the factor of production for sale is their labour, but the same general rule still applies'. (Harvey, op. cit., p. 14.)

To Marxists, Harvey's formulation is nothing but the *reductio ad absurdum* of the whole structure of orthodox economics.

Wages and profits become identified, 'the same rule applies' to both. The class essence of capitalist society, the division of every capitalist community into owners and workers, is totally obscured.

When we say that, in contrast to orthodox economists, Marxists study capitalism dynamically and historically, this must not be taken to mean that orthodox economists do not recognise that, *within* the system, changes do take place with the lapse of time. No orthodox economist would suggest, for example, that conditions in Britain in the 1960s or 1970s are not profoundly different from what they were in the 1930s, but the basic acceptance of private ownership and production for profit has remained unchanged. Moreover, even in the 'public sector' much capital is raised by borrowing from private owners of capital at interest rates determined by capitalist society at large. The large portion of council house rents which goes on interest payments is a case in point. The Marxists are studying the rise and supersession of economic systems, with detailed analysis of the one we happen to be living in. The orthodox are studying the production, exchange and distribution of wealth within a *given* system of property relations. As Marx himself once put it: 'The economists explain the process of production under given conditions; what they do not explain to us, however, is how these conditions themselves are being produced, i.e., the historical movement that brings them into being'. (*Poverty of Philosophy*.) In other words, he does not accuse the orthodox economists of being unscientific within their terms of reference, but of having the wrong terms of reference.

And when we examine the basic reason for this, we cannot avoid facing up to their different class-orientation in society. A system of economic reasoning that accepts private ownership and production for private profit is likely to be acceptable to businessmen and shareholders (at least until they have had a traumatic economic experience). But scientific reasoning that shows that the division of society into workers and drones, or incomes into 'earned' and 'unearned', is not necessarily eternal, and can be replaced by a society in which all able-bodied people work for the community as a whole, will naturally tend to appeal to those who have anyway to live by working.

In neither case can the approach of economists be said to be disinterested; and it is therefore clear why *class* is stressed by Marxists, and also why each side, respectively, accuses the other of being unscientific and subjective.

The Marxists have always the possibility of delivering a Parthian shot by declaring that it is more scientific and more objective to see society as it exists through time than to concentrate on only one stage of its development while ignoring past origins and future possibilities.

To speak of a point of view in economics as being orientated by class allegiance must not be misunderstood as suggesting that every wage-earner is a Marxist or every employer an adherent of orthodox economics. We must recognise that the working class is under a continuous barrage of indoctrination from the capitalist press, advertising, and the mass media aiming to condition people to accept the inevitability of capitalism. Or, as the leading German Marxist Willi Garns recently pointed out: 'Monopoly capitalism tries to make the workpeople believe that they are the co-owners of the means of production'. (*World Marxist Review*, No. 3, 1970.) Hence, just as there are capitalists who are socialists and who even accept Marxist Political Economy, there are a large number of working people who today accept orthodox economics and its judgements.

In such an atmosphere, Marxist Political Economy has always had to conduct a polemical struggle for existence against heavily weighted odds. This has inevitably led to unscientific overstatement from time to time, because polemics can often give rise to emotions uncongenial to cool scientific expression. And, on the other side, we have already seen how orthodox economists, with the security of the Establishment behind them, are liable to become emotionally unscientific as soon as they touch upon Marx, Communism or Socialism.

Neither side, therefore, can present a clean slate as regards consistent objectivity, but the Marxists can at least claim in

c

capitalist countries that their objectivity is likely to be greater since they have no vested interest in preserving the *status quo* and, indeed, may well suffer materially because of their views. They can claim with justification that Galileo in his day was persecuted for his scientific beliefs, beliefs which history has vindicated. And with such examples, they can fortify their morale even against material odds.

Perhaps the first essential point on which the two approaches differ is the subject of Value. It will be well, therefore, to start with this in our examination of the main points of difference.

CHAPTER THREE

Labour, Value and Price

Most people will agree, when we get down to basic principles, that 'utility' or 'use-value' emerges from the activity of men in relation to the free gifts of Nature. Given the raw materials in their natural state, men throughout history have exercised their ingenuity to transform them and to transport them so that their 'utility' or 'use-value' has been created by 'production'. Marx wrote in *Capital* (Vol. I, p. 50), 'material wealth . . . use-values . . . are combinations of two elements—matter and labour . . . As William Petty puts it, labour is the father and the earth its mother'. Therefore, he points out, 'labour is not the only form of material wealth'. The creation of wealth is in fact the result of man's productive activity combined with Nature's 'free gifts'. This proposition of Marx would probably be accepted as a basic truth by orthodox economists; though his obvious corollary, that 'free' gifts cannot have 'value', is certainly not accepted by them.

Marx, unlike the orthodox economists nowadays, logically defined *value* as that which is *added* to Nature's *free* gifts by human labour. When Ricardo showed rent to be a surplus, as a return accruing for the use of a free gift, he was working along similar lines. But contemporary orthodox economics now treats Ricardo as of historical rather than practical importance; which is not surprising when 'land values' are an important feature of the current capitalist way of life.*

* Professor J. R. Hicks accepts this fact to justify the treatment of land for practical purposes nowadays as simply 'a particular kind of capital

Marx also, contrary to popular superstition, did not ignore Demand. His approach was quite clearly stated in the words: 'Ever since the first moment of his appearance on the world's stage, man always has been, and must still be, a consumer, both before and while he is producing'. (Ibid., p. 187.) And again, while stressing that 'value' is the product of the activity known as labour, he made quite clear that goods had to have a use-value, otherwise the labour spent on them would be wasted. So, 'nothing can have value without being an object of utility. If the thing is useless, so is the labour contained in it, the labour does not count as labour, and therefore creates no value'. (Ibid., p. 48.) Hence the concept of *socially necessary* labour, in which demand is implicit.

A further point to note here is that Marx made it clear that if a use-value is itself a *free* gift of nature, it has no 'value' because no human labour has gone into its production. The parallel still recognised by orthodox theory is that, according to Ricardo, pure unimproved land has no cost. Marx makes the point that under competitive conditions price tends towards value, but as items are considered in price which have no value as such, the 'price of production' (or what we would call total 'cost') involves more than just value in most cases. Marx sees the 'possibility' of 'quantitative incongruity between price and magnitude of value, or the deviation of the former from the latter,' as in the case, for example, of 'the price of uncultivated land, which is without value, because no human labour has been incorporated in it'. (Ibid., p. 115.) While the orthodox may criticise Marx's Labour Theory of Value as not being a guide to price, but only an indication of a general tendency; Marxists can, in return, retaliate that the orthodox economist's own concept of 'equilibrium price' which is hardly ever attained, is equally an abstraction. Marx does at times, in certain contexts, identify price and value, but he also makes clear that, generally, price may deviate from value

equipment'. (Hicks, *The Social Framework*, p. 54, fn.) Thus: 'A farmer who rents his land from a landlord is best regarded as paying rent in place of interest'. (Ibid., p. 127, fn.)

because 'prices of production' include prices which do not correspond to values. Thus, while orthodox economics has tended increasingly to identify value with *either* 'utility', 'value-in-use' (or Marx's 'use-value'), *or* 'price', 'value-in-exchange', so the orthodox Theory of Value has increasingly become simply a theory of price determination. As a theory of *price determination* Marx's Labour Theory of Value is of diminishing use as monopoly spreads; but this is not its purpose. Its purpose is to explain how *value* is *created*.

In his actual analysis Marx restricted himself to competitive conditions, under which there is the greatest tendency for price to be held to a level near value. But he never went into the complications which were bound to arise at the monopolistic stage of capitalist development when the tendencies working to keep prices down towards 'value' (Marx) or 'marginal utility' (orthodox school) would cease to operate.

The concept of value as the product of human labour applied to Nature's 'free gifts' is essential to Marx's approach. Its justification lies in the unique quality of labour as *the* productive activity of human beings throughout history, so that the 'creation of value' out of 'Nature's free gifts' is the essence of such activity, and can be measured, whatever the practical difficulties, only by the amount of such activity entailed. Exchange value is therefore basically determined by the conditions of production, though what Marx calls 'accidental' market conditions may cause fluctuations of price at any particular time.

Accepting Marx's proposition that value is the product of human labour, then the only sound comparison of values is the amount of labour used in their production. This approach differs fundamentally from the orthodox, which endows land with value even though it is Nature's 'free' gift, and treats capital as productive, while to Marx it is but a slowly consumed means of production which, like raw materials, are themselves simply the 'crystallised labour' incorporated in them.

While Marx regarded 'socially necessary labour' as the basic criterion in assessing the value of a product, orthodox economists, especially since Marshall, have been content to identify value with price as determined by exchange, including all the factors which Marx regarded as 'accidental', i.e., as not really relating to production of real value at all.

The shift from the concept of 'socially necessary labour', accepted by the classical economists and Marx, to market price, is interestingly explained by Thomas (Lord) Balogh, who writes: 'Under the impact of the use of . . . socially necessary labour . . . by Marx for demonstrating the exploitation of the workers by the propertied classes, the explanation of value by labour was abandoned'. (Balogh, *Unequal Partners*, Vol. I, p. 8.)

This suggestion by Balogh is, in essence, that there is nothing wrong in the Labour Theory of Value in principle, but that it has been inconvenient because of its implications.

Whatever the motives, the fact remains that, from Marshall onwards, instead of scientifically investigating the process by which *use-values* are created by *production*, the attention of orthodox economics has been much more directed to how *prices* (now taken as more or less synonymous with values) are determined by *exchange*. Hence Supply, Demand and Price have become the ubiquitous trinity, applying as much to the supply and demand for the factors of production as to the finished commodities. In such a system no distinction of principle is made between the buying of capital and the buying of labour, except that the type and manner of payment is different. Even profit, within orthodox scheme of things, is just the supply price of enterprise, the 'normal rate of profit' being just that amount which is necessary to keep a firm in a particular line of production. In this sense, 'normal profit' is classed as a cost in no way different, in principle, from wages or salaries.

The fact that the function of 'entrepreneurship' is exercised by owners or their appointed executives, while wages are earned by those who can only offer their services, is glossed over. As Marx himself put the matter: 'Political economy'—in our present context the reference is to orthodox economics—'confuses on principle two very different kinds of private property, of which one rests on the producer's own labour, the other on the employment of the labour of others'. (*Capital*, Vol. I, pp. 838–839.)

Much of Marx's analysis is historical, showing how man's original transformations of nature in ancient times have evolved, by stages, to the present capitalist mode of production. Therefore he gives a detailed account of how common lands in England and clan lands in Scotland were appropriated as private property, both by law and by private actions, one of the most ruthless of all being the Duchess of Sutherland's clearing of 794,000 acres of clan lands of a population which had inhabited them under the ancient Celtic tenure. (Ibid., p. 802.) This 'colonisation' process at home equalled in callousness the many incidents of a similar kind which occurred in the process of building a colonial overseas empire.

The American Paul Baran cites India as an example of which a Marquis of Salisbury once said: 'As India must be bled, the bleeding should be done judiciously'. While, in Baran's view, the total 'volume of wealth that Britain derived from India and that was added to Britain's capital accumulations' has never been fully assessed, he quotes sources for the estimates that 'between £500,000,000 and £1,000,000,000 worth of treasure was taken from India' although the total capital of all joint stock companies operating in India at the turn of the century was no more than £36,000,000. (Baran, *Political Economy of Growth*, p. 145.)

While the agricultural population in Britain was being driven off the land in a series of merciless 'enclosure' movements, capital was accumulating in the hands of merchant traders. This trading, up to the year 1807 in England, included slave trading, from which some of the greatest fortunes were accumulated. At the same time, within Britain itself, a 'traffic in human flesh' took place and poor children were rounded up for the use of the textile employers. (Marx, *Capital*, Vol. I, p. 294.)

Given that labour is the source of value, and that value is therefore only measurable in terms of the amount of *socially necessary* labour embodied in commodities, what is the basis of the value of labour itself, seeing that 'labour-power' is itself a commodity bought by the employers?

Marx makes allowances for differences of skill, but makes the point that his theory is concerned with 'simple average labour', so that skilled labour must be counted as 'multiplied simple labour, a given quantity of skilled labour being considered equal to a greater quantity of simple labour'. (Ibid., p. 51.)

It should also be noted that Marx carefully distinguishes between 'labour' and 'labour-power'. The point is that a worker sells to his employer his *power* to work for a certain period of time. The employers as a class are concerned only with the supply of labour-*power*, and it is this supply which has got to be kept in existence. This 'labour-power or the capacity for labour is to be understood' as 'the aggregate of those mental and physical capabilities existing in a human being, whenever he produces a use-value of any description . . . labour-power can appear on the market as a commodity only if, and so far as, its possessor, the individual whose labour-power it is, offers it for sale, or sells it as a commodity . . . He and the owner of money meet in the market, and deal with each other as on the basis of equal rights, with this difference alone, that one is buyer, the other seller; both, therefore, equal in the eyes of the law'. (Ibid., p. 186.)

'The value of labour-power is determined, as in the case of every other commodity, by the labour-time necessary for the production, and consequently also the reproduction, of this special article . . . the average labour of society incorporated in it . . . the value of labour-power is the value of the means of subsistence necessary for the maintenance of the labourer.' But this is not something static, for Marx points out that 'the number and extent of . . . so-called necessary wants, and also the modes of satisfying them, are themselves the product of historical development, and depend therefore to a great extent on the degree of civilisation of a country, more particularly on the conditions under which, and consequently on the habits and degree of comfort in which, the class of free labourers has been formed.'

There therefore 'enters into the determination of the value of labour-power a historical and moral element'. (Ibid., pp. 189–90.) Also, of course, a sum must be allowed for the costs of training and education as well as for physical reproduction.

The value of labour-power is therefore not static, but can be affected by social practice. Equally, the conditions of work are not something fixed. 'The capitalist maintains his right as a purchaser when he tries to make the working day as long as possible . . . and the labourer maintains his right as a seller when he wishes to reduce the working day to one of definite normal duration. . . Between equal rights force decides. Hence it is that in the history of capitalist production, the determination of what is a working day, presents itself as the result of a struggle . . . between collective capital, i.e., the class of capitalists, and collective labour, i.e., the working class'. (Ibid., p. 259.)

Marx, although in certain passages he pointed to the tendencies in the capitalist system that would lead to the impoverishment of the workers and the enrichment of capital, did not make this a dogma. On the contrary, he clearly foresaw situations in which improved technology would raise the all-round standard of living, benefitting both capitalists and workers. Thus, he wrote, 'it is possible with an increasing productiveness of labour, for the price of labour-power to keep on falling, and yet this fall to be accompanied by a constant growth in the mass of the labourer's means of subsistence.' However, 'the abyss between the labourer's position and that of the capitalist would keep widening'. (Ibid., p. 573.) In other words, the socially necessary items that make up the standard of living of the workers would actually increase at the same time as the accumulation in the hands of the capitalists increased more. Official figures of developments in Britain since the institution of the so-called 'welfare state' suggest that Marx's analysis may now need to be slightly modified, at least in this country, over a very limited historical period. For we find, from official figures (insofar as they are accurate), that in the period from 1959 to 1969 *both* earned incomes (wages and salaries) *and* unearned incomes (profits, rents and surpluses) rose, at not very dissimilar rates. The *Annual Abstract of Statistics* for 1970 gives the following:

	1959	1969
Earned incomes	£14,107 M.	£27,174 M.
Self-employed	1,890 M.	3,009 M.
Profits, Rents, Undistributed surpluses	5,025 M.	9,124 M.

It is true of course that after 1946 some redistribution of income by taxation took place, but this is often much exaggerated.

But the differences are much more striking when we consider, not incomes, but the actual ownership of capital. In 1911–13 92 per cent of the 'personal wealth' of the country was owned by a mere 10 per cent of the population. By 1960 this part of the 'wealth' had fallen to 83 per cent, mainly due to an undoubted increase in small savings and the ownership of housing property by the poorer section. But if we consider the decisive form of capitalist property ownership, 'stocks and shares of companies', we find that as late as 1954 (see Lydall & Tipping, *Bulletin of Oxford University Institute of Statistics*, 1961—a more recent survey has not yet been conducted) the wealthiest 1 per cent of adults owned 81 per cent of the total, while the wealthiest 10 per cent owned 98 per cent of all company stocks and shares. The 'capitalist class' as such could still therefore be quite precisely identified as the proverbial 'upper ten' of the population.

In a speech in 1865, published as *Value, Price and Profit*, Marx went further into the question of the determination of the value of labour-power. He noted that while the minimum was determined by the provision of bare subsistence, there must be considered the 'traditional standard of life' in each country so that while 'we can fix the *minimum* of wages, we cannot fix their *maximum*. We can only say that, the limits of the working day being given, the *maximum of profit* corresponds to the *physical minimum of wages*; and that the wages being given, the *maximum of profit* corresponds to such a prolongation of the working

day as is compatible with the physical forces of the labourer . . .
It is evident that between the two limits . . . an immense scale of
variations is possible. The fixation of the actual degree is only
settled by the continuous struggle between capital and labour'.
Going on further, he comments (over 100 years ago): 'Trades
Unions work well as centres of resistance against the encroach-
ments of capital. They fail partially from an injudicious use of
their power. They fail generally from limiting themselves to a
guerrilla war against the effects of the existing system, instead of
simultaneously trying to change it.' But they have, undoubtedly,
contributed to the raising of the customary minimum standard
of living over the past 100 years to an extent which Marx in his
day did not foresee.

When on the subject of human labour a digression may be
permitted here concerning a term which has acquired a peculiar
ambiguity with the passage of time. This is the distinction between so-called 'productive' and 'unproductive' labour. Marx
differed from Adam Smith on this, and gave the term his own
interpretation which has subsequently not, in fact, been consistently followed by Marxists. In general today both in capitalist
and socialist countries, the prevalent tendency is to identify
'productive labour' with the production of actual material goods,
and 'unproductive labour' with the production of services. This
is consistent with Adam Smith's approach, in which he referred
to 'menial servants' as unproductive.

Marx in one passage in *Capital* (Vol. II, p. 531) has a phrase
which might suggest acceptance of this view when he refers to 'all
so-called unproductive labourers, state officials, physicians,
lawyers, etc.' The contemporary Marxist writer, Oscar Lange,
refers to 'human activities or kinds of labour, such as that of the
artist or teacher, which directly satisfy human needs without
producing material objects or goods . . . they are usually called
non-productive labour'. (Lange, *Political Economy*, Vol 1,
p. 6.)

This interpretation was again repeated in the Soviet newspaper
Pravda in an article by D. Pravdin, which is quite typical, as

recently as 21 September 1971, when he said that 'it is the sectors of the national economy which do not produce material wealth as such that are usually classed under the non-productive sector'. And he listed trade, education and the health service as examples.

In capitalist Britain, at the time that the Selective Employment Tax was introduced, the same distinction was made; the physical production of goods being treated as 'productive' and services to the consumer as 'unproductive'. So this particular distinction, between the production of goods and of services, appears today to be accepted by both socialist and capitalist economists as the distinction between 'productive' and 'unproductive' labour.

But yet another version of 'unproductive labour' has been produced in America by Paul A. Baran, who accepts neither the interpretation given above, nor the formulation of Marx himself which we quote below. Baran, in his *Political Economy of Growth* (pp. 32–3) defines 'unproductive labour' as 'all labour resulting in the output of goods and services the demand for which is attributable to the specific conditions and relationships of the capitalist system, and which would be absent in a rationally ordered society'. This definition enables him to include as 'unproductive' the production of material goods such as 'armaments, luxury articles of all kinds, objects of conspicuous display and marks of social distinction' as well as the 'services' of 'government officials, members of the military establishment, clergymen, lawyers, tax evasion specialists, public relations experts . . . advertising agents, brokers, merchants, speculators, and the like'. He then quotes the authority of Schumpeter for citing also that part of lawyers' activity which 'goes into the struggle of business with the state and its organs'.

It is clear that this interpretation of the meaning of 'unproductive labour' is open to great scope for subjective assessments.

When we come back to what Marx really wrote on the subject we find that none of the above interpretations are his, although this might be thought from one passage in which he describes transport as 'productive' on the ground that it, 'as an industry, sells . . . change of location'. (*Capital*, Vol. II, p. 62.) However, in *Theories of Surplus Value* (Vol. I, p. 388 et seq.), where he goes more fully into the matter, he makes it quite clear that in his sense the terms 'productive' and 'unproductive' labour do not refer to the difference between goods and services at all, but to whether or not the labour is *employed by capital* or *works for itself*. In the former case it yields, in Marx's terminology, 'surplus-value' (See below, Chap. 4), and is thus 'productive'. But in the case of either goods or services which are produced without the intervention of a capitalist, Marx treats such labour as 'unproductive'.

Marx gives the example of a jobbing tailor who makes a pair of trousers for direct purchase by the consumer and he comments: 'The mere *direct* exchange of money for labour therefore does not transform money into capital or labour into productive labour'.

This case is interesting, in that Marx's terminology not only is quite unsuited to orthodox economics, but has in fact in the main been abandoned also by Marxists in favour of the more popular recent usage.

To sum up the essential points so far, then, in Marx's approach to labour, we may enumerate the following:

1. That production is the labour of man applied to the free gifts of nature in order to produce use-values. This is done by transforming their character or transporting them in space.

2. That Marx's distinction between 'productive labour' yielding Surplus-Value and 'unproductive labour' not doing so has been superseded by many economists, including Marxists, who now use the distinction in referring to the difference between producing material goods and producing services.

3. That the only common measure which we have for *values* produced is the amount of socially necessary labour (reduced to a common measure—a unit of unskilled labour) which goes into them.

4. That labour-power, once it is bought and sold as a commodity, is itself valued on average according to the amount of commodities required to keep up its supply.

5. The amount of labour necessary to reproduce the supply of labour-power varies through time, and from country to country, as a result of tradition and Trade Union organisation.

Understood in these terms the Labour Theory of Value still holds water, despite its many critics. But it is not a theory of Price, since Values and Prices can diverge considerably from one another. While Marx rejects the use of the term 'value' for anything not produced by human effort, orthodox economists tend to use the term as increasingly synonymous with price. Even uncultivated land, 'below the margin of cultivation', may have some price and some value to the orthodox economist. But all unimproved land is valueless in Marx's sense, although it may have a price. For it is a 'free' gift of Nature and logically, as a 'free' gift, it is valueless. To Marxists, therefore, the price-system is a superstructure imposed on the more basic value-system; whereas in orthodox economics the Theory of Value, so-called, is nowadays in reality the theory of price determination. To Marx, in contrast, price determination was to a great extent an 'accidental' phenomenon, due to the vagaries of the market.

As far as capital is concerned, Marx treated this as simply 'crystallised labour' used in further production; but he never laid the importance that the orthodox economists do on the difference between 'fixed' and 'working' capital. He recognised the difference as only a matter of degree, the *rate* at which capital was used up in the productive process: 'The coal burnt under a boiler vanishes without leaving a trace. . . . Raw material forms the substance of the product, but only after it has changed its form. Hence raw material and auxiliary substances lose the characteristic form with which they are clothed on entering the labour process.' On the other hand, 'tools, machines, workshops and vessels are of use in the labour-process only so long as they retain their original shape . . . total value is gradually transferred to the product . . . The wear and tear of all instruments, their daily loss of value, and the corresponding quantity of value they part with to the product, are accordingly calculated upon this basis.

'It is thus strikingly clear, that means of production never transfer more value to the product than they themselves lose during the labour-process by the destruction of their own use-value'. (*Capital*, Vol. I, pp. 226–7.)

Marx sharply criticised Adam Smith for 'drowning the distinction between constant and variable capital in that of fixed capital and circulating capital'. (Ibid. Vol. II, pp. 507–8.)

For Marx, the important difference was quite another one: 'the sum of money' which he calls c 'laid out upon the means of production' whether fixed capital or raw materials, and 'the sum of money' which he calls v 'expended upon the labour-power'. (Ibid., Vol. I, p. 235.) In the case of c, whether fixed or working capital (raw materials), the value is transmitted to the product in the course of production. In the case of v, on the other hand, the money is spent on labour-power while the actual labour when employed passes to the product a greater value than is paid for it. Hence the first type of capital is fixed, and is simply passed on to the product; but the second type is variable, in that the value it creates is greater than the amount paid for it.

Not only did Marx criticise Adam Smith for causing confusion by stressing the importance of the difference between fixed and working capital; but he castigated the orthodox approach in general as follows: 'In Capital-Profit, or better Capital-Interest; Land-Rent; Labour-Wages of Labour; in this economic trinity expressing professedly the connection of value and of wealth in general with their sources, we have the complete mystification of the capitalist mode of production . . . This formula corresponds at the same time to the interests of the ruling classes by proclaiming the natural necessity and eternal justification of their sources of revenue and raising them to the position of a dogma'. (Ibid., Vol. III, pp. 966–7.) In fact, says Marx, 'Capital signifies the means of production monopolised by a certain part of society'. Then there is also the land, 'inorganic nature as such, a crude and uncouth mass', and Marx finds it 'remarkable' in orthodox economics that 'Land and Labour are placed indiscriminately by the side of Capital'. (Ibid., pp. 948–9.)

Marx sees the 'capitalist process of production' as a 'historically determined form of the social process of production in general. . . Like all its predecessors, the capitalist process of production takes place under definite material conditions, which are at the same time the bearers of definite social relations'. (Ibid., pp. 952–3.) In these specific social conditions 'capital yields year after year a profit to the capitalist, land a ground-rent to the landlord, and labour-power, under normal conditions and so long as it remains a useful labour-power, a wage to the labourer. These three parts of the total value produced annually . . . are like the annually consumable fruits or a perennial tree, or rather of three trees. They form the annual revenue of three classes, the capitalist, the landlord and the labourer. They are revenues distributed at large by the active capitalist in his capacity as the direct exploiter of surplus labour and employer of labour in general. In this way the capital appears to the capitalist, the land to the landlord, and the labour-power or rather the labour itself, to the labourer . . . as three different sources of their respective revenues, of profits, ground-rent and wages'. (Ibid., pp. 956–7.)

On this 'appearance' rests the entire structure of traditional orthodox economics. Indeed, since Marx wrote these words (edited posthumously by Engels in 1894) there has been very little alteration to the basic concept of factors of production, except that to Land, Labour and Capital a fourth category has since been added: Enterprise—for which the return may be broadly called Profit. But the interweaving of the concepts of interest and profit (Dividend interest being paid out of profits, only debenture interest being real interest and so on) has become so complicated that it is now hard to find any two orthodox economists who treat the matter in the same way.

Orthodox economists, taking for granted the private ownership of land and capital, accept as a dogma that the means of production remain private property except in the 'public sector'. And, in so far as any of these 'factors of production' are supplied for the productive process, their return is decided by the interaction of Supply and Demand. Marx does not deny that this is what happens in capitalist society, but he does deny that this sort of analysis lays bare the essence of the situation, and he denies that the state of affairs described has anything but a transitory character in human history.

Paul Sweezy, in his *Theory of Capitalist Development*, draws attention to the fact that Marx's 'total value is equivalent to gross receipts from sales, constant capital to outlay on materials plus depreciation, variable capital to outlay on wages and salaries, and surplus value (which we deal with in the next chapter) 'to income available for distribution as interest and dividends or for reinvestment in the business. Marx's value theory thus has the great merit, unlike some other value theories, of close correspondence to the actual accounting categories of capitalistic business enterprise'. (Sweezy, op. cit., p. 63.) And, as we have already mentioned, his emphasis on labour being the real source of value is surprisingly in accord with the British Inland Revenue's conception of 'earned' as against 'unearned' incomes.

Nowadays, when the replacement of capital goods tends to become increasingly rapid, we have many cases of capital goods being scrapped because they are 'technologically obsolete' long before they have ceased to be usable in production; i.e. long before they have yet fully passed on their value to products. In such cases we must regard their value as having been wasted, and the labour that went to produce them, though paid for, has subsequently turned out not to have been 'socially necessary'. In practice, of course, firms do not scrap equipment unless they calculate that they will be compensated for the waste involved by the greater labour productivity made possible by the substitution of the new equipment.

Accepting Marx's historical approach to capitalism, it cannot be denied that the expropriation of the peasants from the land—both at home and in the colonies; the accumulation of merchant capital to a great extent through the slave trade; the near-slave conditions in which children were employed in industry in the early stages of the Industrial Revolution; were all means of capital accumulation which had nothing whatever to do with

D

'free' bargaining between equals on the basis of the interaction of Supply, Demand and Price. When orthodox writers refer scornfully to Marx's laborious use of statistics and Blue Books and Parliamentary reports covering the whole period of England's Industrial Revolution, they overlook the fact that all this was necessary to provide the historical data to show that there is no more a Divine Right to private property than there is a Divine Right of Kings.

We live today under a system in which the 'profit motive' is said to be supreme. This can be rationalised into a system in which profit is a return, or reward, for certain social functions called business enterprise or risk-taking. But if we recognise that, historically, and basically even today, it is labour which creates value, where does the profit come from? We examine this question in the following chapter.

CHAPTER FOUR

The Source of Profit

We have already seen that a fundamental difference between the Marxist and the orthodox approach to economics lies in the different conceptions of the meaning of 'value'. To Marx it is the result of human labour acting on the 'free gifts of nature'. And this labour may be direct, or it may be 'crystallised' in machinery or raw materials and passed on to the product slowly or rapidly during the production process.

Marx is careful not to identify price with value completely, though he does describe it as 'the money-name of the labour realised in a commodity'. But this is only a tendency, for 'as soon as magnitude of value is converted into price' this becomes 'a more or less accidental exchange-ratio between a single commodity and another, the money commodity' and there may be, as we have seen (*supra*, p. 38), 'quantitative incongruity between price and the magnitude of value'. (*Capital*, Vol. I, pp. 114–15.)

Moreover, as we saw in the last chapter, certain things have prices even though they have no value, and these can enter into costs, or Marx's 'price of production'. Thus in Vol. III Marx defines 'price of production' in a way consistent with the contemporary orthodox concept of 'cost of production' including 'normal rate of profit'. Marx writes that 'price of production of a commodity' is 'equal to its cost-price plus the average profit' (Op. cit., Vol. III, p. 186.)

Marx also saw that prices fluctuated as a result of market conditions, monopoly, and other factors which he termed 'accidental', in an analysis which assumed competitive conditions. He also noted variations in the value of money and wrote:

'A general rise in the prices of commodities can result only, either from a rise in their values—the value of money remaining constant—or from a fall in the value of money, the values of commodities remaining constant'. (Ibid., Vol. I, p. 111.) It is therefore possible for prices to depart considerably from an accurate measure of values, and Marx, while considering competitive capitalism as tending to keep prices in the neighbourhood of values, never went into what would happen when the capitalist economy became dominated by monopolies on a large scale.

While recognising that, as between firms, there may be considerable differences in profit at any one time, Marx assumed that as a result of competition, rates of profit would tend to equalise in the long run. But whence, when we probe more deeply, comes this profit?

In orthodox economics, profit is the return for 'enterprise' and 'risk-taking' and the businessman has a right to his profit as the price for his contribution to production. In such a scheme of things, the source of profit is the 'wage' of good management, good business forecasting, and successful risk-taking. The basic difference between 'earned income' and 'unearned income' is only recognised in orthodox economics when dealing with taxation. Moreover, since profit is the 'return' for risk-taking and enterprise, a 'normal rate of profit' is accepted as being as much a cost of production as wages. To call forth the necessary supply of labour the demand price (wage offered) must be adequate. To call forth the necessary supply of enterprise and capital the demand prices (normal rate of profit and interest) must be offered. In this picture both the suppliers of labour owning no capital and the owners of businesses and suppliers of capital are treated as being on the same footing. Marx rejects this on the ground that the one group *has* to live by supplying its labour-power, whereas, on the other hand, the second group *owns* the means of production and therefore has the right to employ or discharge the labour of others according to the criterion of profitability.

In the orthodox theory, suppliers of capital provide the service of 'waiting', 'abstinence' or 'foregoing liquidity', for which they are paid interest. But Marx points out that it is only a convenient assumption for the capitalists that abstinence from spending should be rewarded. For to Marx, accumulation of wealth is a positive satisfaction to the capitalist, and the building up of his capital is an aim of his economic life as important as consumption. In so far as capitalists *want* both to consume *and* to accumulate, says Marx, there is no logic in paying them for one and charging them for the other.

The abstinence theory is a convenient explanation of interest, for those who accept the system and accept the idea that it should be perpetuated. But it is based on the essentially false assumption that capitalists do not wish to save and invest. The orthodox procedure of 'marginal analysis' covers up this fact, since while *at the margin* the rate of return may indeed determine in which direction new business activity or new capital will flow, the marginal rate, as is well known, bears little relationship to the total. The investment of capital as a whole can perfectly well yield a positive satisfaction to the investors and yet, *at the margin of investment*, a material incentive may be necessary to decide these same capitalists whether to invest in one scheme or another (i.e. the 'transfer costs' of modern orthodoxy). Marx's dismissal of interest as such, as not being necessary to ensure saving and investment, is not inconsistent with the orthodox analysis by which, *at the margin*, interest may play a decisive role once the system is accepted.

Hence, to Marx, both profit and interest arise from surplus-value extracted by those who own the means of production in the course of employing those who have to sell their labour-power in order to live. An 'essential condition to the owner of money finding labour-power in the market as a commodity is this—that the labourer instead of being in the position to sell commodities in which his labour is incorporated, must be obliged to offer for sale as a commodity that very labour-power, which exists only in his living self' while the 'owner of money . . . regards the labour market as a branch of the general market for commodities. . . .

One thing, however, is clear—nature does not produce on the one side owners of money or commodities, and on the other men possessing nothing but their own labour-power. This relation has no natural basis, neither is its social basis one that is common to all historical periods. It is clearly the result of a past historical development'. (Ibid., Vol. I, pp. 187–8.) And Marx devotes much space to the study of this development.

Now labour-power is sold at its value, that is, as we have seen, the socially accepted means of subsistence necessary to produce and reproduce it. It is this labour-power, 'capacity for labour', which is sold to the employer. To take the simplest sort of example from the good old days of 1867: A labourer received 3s. a day for his labour-power, and 'six hours labour are incorporated in that sum' because this was the 'amount of labour . . . requisite to produce the necessaries of life daily required on an average by the labourer'. Now if the working day was twelve hours, only six of them have been worked by the labourer for himself, and six for his employer. 'The fact that half a day's labour was necessary to keep the labourer alive during twenty-four hours, does not in any way prevent him from working a whole day. Therefore the value of labour-power, and the value which that labour-power creates in the labour process, are two entirely different magnitudes; and this difference of the two values was what the capitalist had in view when he was purchasing the labour-power. . . . What really influenced him was the specific use-value which this commodity possesses of being a *source not only of value, but of more value than it has itself.* This is the special service that the capitalist expects from labour-power, and in this transaction he acts in accordance with the "eternal laws" of the exchange of commodities.' (Ibid., pp. 215–16.)

Thus, in employment, labour-power is paid its value, which is enough to ensure its supply at existing social standards and conventions. But in the working day it produces more value than it has been paid. This extra value is what Marx calls 'surplus-value' and is the source of profit, interest and rent that accrue to the property-owning class as a whole.

It should be noted that, although Marx's examples were worked out on the basis of conditions prevailing in the middle of the last century, it is still a common practice among militant trade unionists to calculate their wages per head and, balanced against this, profits per head of labour employed. They are in fact using near-Marxist techniques in doing this, for they are recognising that every day's work has produced enough to pay for wages and other costs plus the surplus which is termed profit.

A recent example of how this works out in practice was given by the late Emile Burns in his *Money and Inflation* (1968) where he cited a 1966 report on the Ford Motor Company, where 'between 1962 and 1965 the annual production of vehicles per worker rose from 11.7 to 15.6—a productivity increase of 32 per cent. Sales per worker rose from £6,200 to £9,200—a rise of 48 per cent. But hourly wages had risen by only 15.5 per cent for grade 1 workers, and 14 per cent for grade 2 workers. During these years the company had been able to put over £35 million out of gross profits into reserves'. (Op. cit., p. 39.)

While this quotation stresses one aspect, we should not forget that, in any large firm at any particular time, selling price may be above value, and above what might be considered a reasonable competitive price. In the car industry we have many instances of partial monopoly associated with exclusive models and so on, and in the circumstances cited above there may have well been an element of monopoly profit for Ford owing to market conditions. Marx tended to ignore exceptional profits due to current market conditions as 'accidental', but in these days when monopoly plays such a decisive part in capitalism we must recognise that the reaping of profit from selling goods above their value as a result of monopolistic or semi-monopolistic conditions is now characteristic.

But whether we assume competitive conditions, which Marx did in his analysis in depth of the creation of value, or monopoly as it exists today in so many decisive sectors of the capitalist economic system, as Marx forecast that it would do, in either case money is used by those that have it in order to employ labour for less than the value of its contribution to production, thus yielding the surplus-value out of which comes profit as the motive force of the capitalist system.

In real life, of course, profits often arise without employing labour: Profits from buying cheap and selling dear; profits arising from monopoly; profits from speculation in such non-productive fields as stocks and shares and land prices; but Marx treated these as 'accidental', arising out of market conditions, in which, in the main, one capitalist's gain is another capitalist's loss. The *nett* profits accruing to the capitalists as a whole he saw as the result of the sharing out among the property-owners as a whole of the surplus-value resulting from the exploitation of all labour in production.

In the case of monopoly profits, these too were seen by Marx as mainly the enrichment of one section of the capitalists at the expense of another. But had he lived today, he would undoubtedly have noted the extent to which monopolies are supplying consumers (usually disguising their products under a legion of different brand names), so that taken as a whole monopoly price-fixing is adversely affecting the cost of living, has become a widely prevalent means of effectively reducing the purchasing power of money wages, and is causing chronic 'inflation'.

Just as orthodox economics sees no difference in principle between the supply and demand for labour and the supply and demand for 'enterprise' and capital, so, too, it sees no difference in kind between profit derived from the employment (Marx's 'exploitation') of labour, and profit derived from fluctuations in prices. The entire trend in the direction of market analysis tends to confuse the two, while Marx's aim was to preserve the distinction between them.

If we take Marx's starting point, that historically there is nothing sacrosanct in private property, and that its origin and evolution form a long story of conquest and confiscation, the extraction of surplus-value by the exploitation of wage-labour becomes simply the latest in a series of social systems, including slavery and serfdom, dependent on the exploitation of the majority by a property-owning minority. If it can be shown that the capitalist system itself is unstable, and in fact paving the way for some other social and economic system which would eliminate its basic internal conflicts, then, says Marx, this is the solution towards which history is moving.

But this will not just come about automatically. Class interests are involved in preserving private ownership, just as other class interests are involved in wishing to replace it by common ownership. Moreover, capitalism itself, by bringing together large numbers of workers in industrial enterprises, and in obliging them to develop trade unionism to defend their interests, is training the working class in collective working and collective organisation of precisely the kind which is necessary to run a socialist society. This is not—as is so often suggested—a faith in any ethical 'superiority' of the working class; but simply a realistic appraisal of a class trained and accustomed to collective and co-operative activity as against the class of capitalists trained to be ruthless competitors on the principle of dog eat dog. This basic difference between the social background of the workers and the social background of the capitalists is not vitiated by the fact that, on matters of detail, such as demarcation disputes between unions, there may be differences at times between particular groups of workers themselves.

As we have seen, Marx distinguished between two types of capital, but his distinction was not that which is made by the orthodox economists. All capital that passed on its value to the product, whether quickly or slowly, was constant capital, c, in Marx's analysis. But that which was used to employ labour, which gave more value to the product than was paid in wages, was treated as the variable element, v. If a worker 'earned' his wage in six hours and then worked six hours for the benefit of his employer, the variable capital v paid in wages would produce a surplus-value of the equivalent amount, s, so that the *rate of surplus value* would be s/v, in this example 100 per cent (*Capital*, Vol. I, p. 331.) Marx distinguished also the *mass* of surplus value, as the *rate* multiplied by the amount of variable capital in use, i.e. $s/v \times v$, which brings us back to s, the total surplus-value gained from the operation.

Marx in his day drew a distinction, within the category of surplus-value itself, between 'absolute' and 'relative'. The former he ascribed to the result of increasing the working day of given average intensity, i.e., the time spent by the worker in working for the employer and not for himself. There was always an absolute limit to this in the maximum working day of which a worker was physically capable. Today this has become subject both to legal and trade union control and is no longer of great importance in developed countries.

The second possibility, of 'surplus value arising from the curtailment of the necessary labour-time,' an 'increase in the productiveness of labour . . . of such a kind as to shorten the labour-time socially necessary for the production of a commodity, and to endow a given quantity of labour with the power of producing a greater quantity of use-value', is what is now primarily important in every developed capitalist country. This necessitates that 'the technical and social conditions of the process, and consequently the very mode of production must be revolutionised, before the productiveness of labour can be increased'. (Ibid., p. 345.)

There may be a curtailment of the necessary labour-time spent in production of a certain quantity of a product, and there also may be a fall in the 'value of labour-power' (i.e. cost of living) itself if the increase in productivity affects those branches of industry supplying the needs of the labourer (assuming, of course, a competitive reduction in prices to keep pace with the increase in productivity). But the value of labour-power will itself be undisturbed if 'an increase in the productiveness of labour' is in 'those branches of industry which supply neither the necessaries of life, nor the means of production for such necessaries'. (Ibid., p. 346.)

So 'relative surplus value' arising from increased productivity may take the form of (a) a given number of average working hours yielding a larger product, so that the proportion of output which takes the form of surplus value is higher, or (b) a fall in the cost of the means of subsistence (assuming that it is passed on to the consumer) so that the value of labour power, the cost of living, itself falls, and again the proportion of output which takes the form of surplus value is higher. Marx concludes: 'The object of all development of the productiveness of labour, within the limits of capitalist production, is to shorten that part of the working day, during which the workman must labour for his own benefit, and by that very shortening, to lengthen the other part of the day, during which he is at liberty to work for the capitalist'. (Ibid., p. 352.)

It should be noted that, in contemporary Britain, where monopolistic policies aiming at restricting supplies to keep up prices are prevalent, so-called 'productivity agreements' can hit the workers in another way. If, for example, a productivity agreement were guaranteed to raise production proportionately, with appropriate reductions in price to the consumer, it could be argued that such agreements were in the interest of the community. But this usually does not happen. The agreement increases *productivity per head*, but firms do not raise their output proportionately. They sack 'redundant' workers instead; thus preserving the same flow of supplies at existing (or rising) prices ✗ to the consumer, while economising on their wages bill even if they pay to the workers retained a somewhat higher wage than before. This is typical of the operation of 'productivity agreements' under monopoly capitalism, and it is clear why they are regarded with the utmost suspicion by most trade unionists.

Workers do, of course, often find ways and means of improving their economic position. The worker who does 'odd jobs' may not only increase his income thereby, but may find a way of supplying his labour direct to the consumer without the intervention of a capitalist profiting at his expense. Marx noted such cases, and it was these which he termed 'unproductive labour', not producing surplus value. Again, as a result of collective bargaining, most workers now get paid overtime, which means that, on the extra hours, the rate of surplus value is lower.

Marx also spent considerable time on what is now known in

orthodox terminology as 'economies of scale', bringing more and more workers into schemes entailing the Division of Labour. He quotes John Stuart Mill's dictum on mechanisation: 'It is questionable if all mechanical inventions yet made have lightened the day's toil of any human being' and in a footnote adds the comment: 'Mill should have said "of any human being not fed by other people's labour"'. (Ibid., p. 405.)

In these days in Britain, when redundancy is mounting to mass unemployment once again, it is worthy of note that Marx always saw redundancy and unemployment as inherent in capitalism itself. He drew attention to the contradiction between 'technical necessities' and the 'social character' of modern industry, which 'dispels all fixity and security in the situation of the labourer . . . constantly threatens, by taking away his instruments of labour, to snatch from his hands the means of subsistence, and, by suppressing his detail-function, to make him superfluous'. (Ibid., p. 533.) The return to mass unemployment in Britain, after a honeymoon of twenty-five years, simply brings us back to the reality as outlined by Marx after a long period of fantasy-spinning around the phenomenon of 'full employment'.

While Marx saw surplus-value as the basic source of profit, he recognised that its actual *rate*, and the rate of profit too, might vary enormously. He calculated the rate of surplus value (s/v) on the veriable capital only, i.e. the amount spent on labour power; but he calculated the rate of *profit* on the *total* capital C, which is c and v together. His rate of profit was therefore $s/c+v$. It follows from this that if the proportion of constant to variable capital increases and the rate of surplus value remains constant, then the *rate of profit* must fall. The increase of constant capital as a proportion of the total is a general tendency under capitalism, c/v grows, or, as Marx puts it, the 'organic composition of capital' increases. So long as variable capital grows more slowly than constant capital—a tendency to more capital-intensive production, and the *rate* of surplus value remains constant, then the surplus value will rise more slowly than the total volume of capital (constant and variable together), and therefore, if the rate of

THE SOURCE OF PROFIT

surplus value does not change, the rate of profit on total capital
will inevitably fall. Marx put it this way: 'If you take any quantity of the average social capital, say a capital of 100, you will
find that an ever larger portion of it is vested in means of production and an ever smaller proportion in living labour'. (Ibid.,
Vol. III, p. 252.) This does not mean that the sum total of
profits may not still be growing, but it does mean that if s/v
remains constant the *rate of profit per unit* of capital tends to fall.
There is therefore simultaneously 'an increase in the absolute
mass of profit and a falling rate of profit'. (Ibid., p. 256.)

The growth of constant capital relative to labour also has
repercussions on the demand for labour—our familiar redundancy. The additional capital formed in the course of accumulation
attracts fewer and fewer labourers in proportion to its magnitude.
On the other hand, the old capital periodically reproduced with
change of composition repels more and more of the labourers
formerly employed by it.' Hence the growth of 'a relative surplus
population or industrial reserve army'. (Ibid., Vol. I, p. 689.)
This leads to 'a disproportion between the growing increase of
capital and its relatively decreasing demand for an increase in
population'. (Ibid., Vol. III, p. 260.) In these days of concern
throughout the capitalist world about the so-called 'population
explosion' these words of Marx are prophetic. And, before
accepting uncritically all that is said today about the 'population
explosion' it is worth while at least to ask just how far this is a
reflection of the ideology of capitalism and how far it is really
justified if considered from the point of view of a rational distribution of wealth and resources on a world scale.

The emphasis given by Marx and many of his followers to the
'falling rate of profit' rests on the assumption that the rate of
surplus value remains constant. But does it in real life? Marx
himself enumerated a number of counterbalancing causes which
in fact left only a *tendency* for the rate of profit to fall. These
countervailing tendencies included more intensive exploitation of
labour, the depression of wages below their value (nowadays
done to a far greater extent than was foreseen by Marx by attacks

on real wages through rising prices), and the 'cheapening of the elements of constant capital'. But above all, nowadays, tendencies for the rate of profit to fall are offset, in a large part of industry, by monopolistic price-raising above what could reasonably be expected under conditions of competition.

Even among those who are in general appreciative of Marx's approach, doubts have been expressed about his 'falling rate of profit'. Baran, Sweezy and Joan Robinson have all expressed such doubts on the ground that such a falling rate of profit has not come about.

But it would seem here that an incorrect interpretation is being placed on what Marx was getting at. If, for example, we consider today such capital-intensive enterprises as atomic power stations, hydro-electric stations, and much of the oil and chemical industries which employ very little labour in proportion to capital, we find that—unless they can compensate themselves through *charging monopolistic prices*—they are *not profitable* by ordinary capitalist standards. Therefore they are dependent either on state support or on monopolistic price policies. These cases do, in fact, vindicate Marx's view.

And indeed it is rather surprising to find that J. M. Keynes, for all his contempt for Marx (see *supra*, p. 17), wrote as follows in his major work: 'I feel sure that the demand for capital is strictly limited in the sense that it would not be difficult to increase the stock of capital up to a point where its marginal efficiency had fallen to a very low figure. This would not mean that the use of capital instruments would cost almost nothing, but only that the return from them would have to cover little more than their exhaustion by wastage and obsolescence together with some margin to cover risk and the exercise of skill and judgement. In short . . . just cover their labour-costs of production plus an allowance for risk and the costs of skill and supervision'. (Keynes, *General Theory of Employment, Interest and Money*, p. 375.)

In point of fact, Keynes did not penetrate as deeply as Marx, for he never perceived that (a) in admitting the ease with which capital could be called forth, he was confirming Marx's view that basically, to capitalists, to invest has *utility* and not disutility, and (b) that the reason behind the 'falling marginal efficiency' of capital is a fall in its *profitability* from employing labour, and has nothing to do with efficiency in the technical sense.

At the time Marx was writing, competitive capitalism was still the norm. And in his analysis of value he assumed competitive conditions in which prices would tend to be held down in the direction of values, and profits would be averaged out among the capitalists in the course of competition. In making such assumptions, Marx was doing no more than orthodox economists do when they assume that competition will keep prices down to marginal costs *except* in cases of monopoly.

But as monopoly has become typical of the whole system, and finance and banking have also become monopolised and have enormously increased the role of credit in the economy, it has become possible for monopoly capitalism, with its simultaneous control both of finance and industry, to use 'inflation' as a means of cutting real incomes at the very time that trade unions are causing money incomes to rise. In such conditions the working class (a) still produces more than it is paid for at the point of production, and in addition is (b) systematically charged prices for the means of consumption which are above their values.

If, in 1971, we consider contemporary Britain, we find that crises in a whole range of enterprises may be put down to the 'falling rate of profit' in Marx's sense, expressed, in orthodox terms, as forms of over-capitalisation. In privately-owned industry we have had the cases of Rolls Royce, the Upper Clyde Shipbuilders and BSA. While in each case specific causes may be named for the crisis, basically it is hard to maintain that these are not all phenomena arising from the steady growth of constant capital that has to be invested in modern industry, and the 'falling rate of profit' arising from such investment. The steady tendency for government to have to support modern large-scale enterprises is another symptom of the same general tendency.

It follows that, like the 'impoverishment of the working class', the 'falling rate of profit' is a tendency at work within capitalism.

It can be offset in its visible effects by improvements in techniques, monopoly, and state aid to private industry. But as recent events have shown, not only in Britain but on a world scale with the dollar crisis, the instability of the system, due to the opposing tendencies within it, continues.

In orthodox economics much time is spent on analysing the 'Distribution' of incomes among the suppliers of the 'Factors of production'. This was also true in Marx's day, but while the orthodox treated all suppliers equally, Marx stressed the essential difference as being between those who produced and those who appropriated surplus-value. 'Capital', he wrote, 'is not only, as Adam Smith says, the command over labour. It is essentially the command over unpaid labour. All surplus-value, whatever particular form (profit, interest or rent) it may subsequently crystallize into, is in substance the materialisation of unpaid labour. The secret of the self-expansion of capital resolves itself into having the disposal of a definite quantity of other people's unpaid labour.' (*Capital*, Vol. I, p. 585.) In *Capital*, Vol. II, Marx goes into detail concerning this distribution of surplus-value among the property owners, discussing interest and profit in Part V and ground-rent in Part VI.

Marx thus sees dealings in property, whether land or capital, as conducted by the property owners themselves in sharing out the surplus value which has accrued to them from somebody else's labour. Suppose, for example, that an employer has produced goods 'with his own capital'. In this case 'he pockets the whole surplus'. But if he has borrowed the capital, he may have to give up' so much 'for interest. This does not alter anything in the value of the 'product', but only in the distribution of the surplus-value . . . between different persons'. (*Capital*, Vol. III, p. 407.)

A contemporary parallel to this is to be seen in the raising of capital for joint stock companies. If, say, £100,000 is raised by the issue of Ordinary Shares, the dividend on this capital is paid out of 'profits'. But if exactly the same sum, £100,000 is raised by issuing Debentures, even if it is spent on exactly the same capital equipment, interest is paid out of the 'cost' of the company. If, today, ordinary capitalist practice draws such an ambiguous line between 'profits' and 'costs'; who is to dispute Marx's view that there is no essential difference between rent, interest and profit because they are all aspects of the same Surplus-Value?

Marx also had some interesting things to say about the classical 'entrepreneur', the owner-manager of a business. 'In distinction from interest', he wrote, 'his profit of enterprise appears to him as independent of the ownership of capital, it seems to be the result of his function as a non-proprietor—*a labourer.*

'Under these circumstances the brain necessarily conceives the idea, that his profit of enterprise, far from being in opposition to wage-labour and representing only the unpaid labour of others, is rather itself *wages of labour*, wages of superintendence of labour. These wages are superior to those of the common labourer, (1) because they pay more for more complicated labour, (2) because the capitalist pays them to himself.' (Ibid., p. 447.)

Lest Marx be accused of over-simplification here, it should be noted that he did not ignore the actual labour entailed in the functions of organisation and management. The owner-manager of a business, said Marx, 'creates surplus-value, not because he performs *the work of a capitalist*, but because he *also* works aside from his capacity as a capitalist'. It follows that 'a portion of the profit may indeed be separated, and is separated in reality, as wages, or rather the reverse, that a portion of the wages appear under capitalist production as a separate portion of the profit. Already Adam Smith indicated, that this portion assumes its pure form, independently of profit and wholly separated from it . . . in the salary of the superintendent in those lines of business, whose size, etc., permits a sufficient division of labour to justify a special salary for the labour of a superintendent . . . a kind of productive labour, which must be performed in every mode of production requiring a combination of labours'. (Ibid., pp. 450–1.) This remark, incidentally, might well be pondered by those 'socialist' or anarchist critics of the socialist countries who see a contradiction in the use of managerial personnel.

E

So, in reckoning the origins of surplus-value, Marx did not ignore that particular category of income which may be termed the wages of administration. Moreover, he noted that 'compared to the money-capitalist the industrial capitalist is a labourer, but a labouring capitalist, an exploiter of the labour of others'. (Ibid., p. 455.) In contrast to such a situation he posed the possibility of a co-operative factory in which 'the antagonistic character of the labour of superintendence disappears, since the manager is paid by the labourers instead of representing capital against them'. (Ibid., p. 456.)

He went on: 'The confounding of the profit of enterprise with the wages of superintendence or management was due originally to the antagonistic form assumed toward interest . . . It was further promoted by the apologetic intention to represent profit, not as a surplus-value derived from unpaid labour, but as wages of the capitalist himself for labour performed by him'. (Ibid., p. 457.) Lastly, 'a new swindle develops in stock enterprises with the wages of management. It consists in placing above the actual director a board of managers or directors, for whom superintendence and management serve in reality only as a pretext for plundering stockholders and amassing wealth'. He gave an example of 'bankers and merchants . . . being on the boards of eight or nine different companies', and cited the example of one of them who 'showed an income of 8,000 pounds a year under the head of directorships. . . . The proceedings of the court of bankruptcy show, that these wages of superintendence are as a rule inversely proportioned to the actual superintendence performed by these nominal directors'. (Ibid., pp. 458–9.)

Compared with present-day magnitudes, Marx's example now seems rather modest. The *Sunday Times* of 1 November, 1970, featured a number of Britain's 'top earners' among the chairmen of joint stock companies: Annual salaries were listed, together with, in brackets, the amount left after tax. The following are examples: David Barran, Shell, £72,809 (£13,800); John Clark, Plessey, £66,653 (£13,100); Sir Peter Allen, ICI, £57,915 (£12,200) and so forth. Whether the quantity and quality of labour put into superintendence and management would justify such sums in any rationally organised economic system is left to the reader's judgement.

It has been fashionable to describe Marx as out-of-date. But allowing for an astronomical rise in the salaries of chairmen and members of boards of directors since Marx's day, his words appear to be as apt now as when they were written.

While Marx as a rule was dealing with average rates of profit arising from surplus-value, he also recognised what he described as 'surplus-profit' resulting from 'mere transactions in the sphere of circulation, of mere fluctuations of market prices' and from the use of some 'natural agency of production' such as a water-fall for power. (*Capital*, Vol. III, p. 753.) While waterfalls are obviously 'free gifts of nature', in so far as they are privately owned they can claim a share of surplus-profit in the form of ground rent.

Again, there are 'fluctuations of profit due to the cycle of fat and lean years'. And there also takes place a process of 'continually transferring capital from one sphere to another, in which the profit happens to stand above the average for the moment. . . These incessant immigrations and emigrations of capital, which take place between the different spheres of production, create rising and falling movements of the rate of profit' which 'balance one another more or less and thereby create a tendency to reduce the rate of profit everywhere to the same common and universal level'. (Ibid., p. 243.)

Yet one other factor which can raise profits abnormally is monopoly, which we have already mentioned, and which Marx wrote 'may enable either of the contracting sides to sell commodities above their value or compel others to sell below value'. (Ibid., p. 209.) What Marx did not do was to analyse what would happen to the relationship between prices and values, always rather tenuous, when monopolistic price-fixing became a built-in feature of the system. Whereas, under competition, profits tended to be equalised, this is no longer true when monopolies dominate the system. For now, by their own monopolistic price policy, the monopoly capitalists can not only gain extra profit at the expense of the workers' living standards, but also at the expense of fellow capitalists who are unable to climb to the privileged position which monopoly provides. In this situation there is a basis for a political popular front of all who suffer exploitation by the monopolies.

The strength of the trade union movement in the developed countries since 1946, and the political changes which it has helped to bring about, have obliged capitalist states to introduce certain conscious controls which undoubtedly for twenty-five years helped to keep unemployment at bay. Fear of social unrest has itself become a factor inducing capitalist states to check in some degree the natural urges of capitalism. But world events in the past two years have shown both British 'full employment' and the supremacy of the dollar to have been not permanent 'miracles' but transitory phenomena.

On 22 May 1971, *The Economist* reported that 'as a result of past deficits' in the USA's trading balance, 'at least $40 billion' were in foreign hands at a time when the gold reserves of the Federal Reserve Bank were no more than $11 billion. Hence the inconvertibility and at last the devaluation of this 'reserve currency' had become inevitable. Against this background it is ironical to recall that in the 1920s, before the World Economic Crisis, J. M. Keynes (as he then was) used satirically to conjure up the eternal prospect of gold being laboriously mined in South Africa only to be transported and laboriously buried again in the vaults of the Federal Reserve Bank. Even Keynes did not foresee the world economic crisis, nor the accumulation by the USA of a balance of payments deficit in the years following its disastrous launching of war against Vietnam.

The fact is that, despite his derogatory attitude to Marx, Keynes never got beyond the manipulation of money *within* capitalism and was therefore oblivious of the fatal weaknesses inherent in the system itself. Mattick puts it vividly when he writes: 'The Keynesians see the economy as a money economy and tend to forget that it is a *money-making* economy'. To the

Keynesians, he says, 'money appears as a mere instrument of manipulation for turning insufficient into sufficient social production . . . there must be the *right* quantity of money; and it is the government's function to arrange for this *right quality*'. (Mattick, *Marx and Keynes*, p. 169).*

In the countries of 'free enterprise' and the 'free market', competition has gradually had to surrender to the rise of monopolies, often interlocking, often ruthlessly competing against one another, and often posing before the general public as being non-existent by trading under many names and even at times allowing these to advertise against each other as if they were independent. And the main characteristic of monopoly is, both to the Marxist and to the orthodox economist, its tendency to charge prices above 'value' (Marx) or 'marginal cost' (orthodoxy).

This does not mean that every monopoly, in every situation, will pursue a high price policy. One of the characteristics of monopoly capitalism is the unevenness of its development, and the position of one single company may vary greatly from country to country, market to market, in regard to its monopolistic potentialities. Ability to pursue a high price policy depends on a lack of substitutes to which the consumer may turn; and when the competition of substitutes is present a monopolist may have, at least for a time, to pursue a low price policy until the rival is defeated.

Nevertheless, the tendency towards ever greater monopolies continues, financed by giant banks and financial companies, themselves enjoying monopoly privileges in certain spheres. The resultant inflation of prices is, in capitalist countries, invariably pilloried as an effect of unreasonable wage demands on the part of the workers. 'Prices and Incomes Policies' are now of international concern in the capitalist countries, and in all cases they are directed primarily against wages, i.e. *earned* incomes, and not against unearned incomes and prices. This itself confirms the fact that under monopoly capitalism the state operates

---

* It remains a mystery how one who so correctly pinpoints the essence of Keynesianism could at the same time allege that the socialist planned economies are 'Keynesian'. (See below, p. 153.)

primarily in the interests of monopoly capital, and even a Labour Government in Britain showed itself an enthusiast for mergers and take-overs, inevitably leading to greater concentrations of capital thereby making competition less and less possible. The fact that large monopolistic concerns have been so keen on backing Britain's entry into the Common Market gives reason to believe that it is the large monopolistic capitalist concerns that really stand to gain. It was revealing that the usually 'pro-Market' *Economist*, on 26 June 1971, noted 'a good deal of nervousness in the business community' about joining, and it went on to elaborate where support really lay. 'Throughout the year,' it wrote, 'the chemical industry has devoted its lobbying activities to pushing for Common Market entry. Imperial Chemical Industries is still Europe's largest producer'. Again, in textiles, with 'the growing dominance of the big groups like Courtaulds and ICI' (between whom a forthcoming marriage was subsequently widely rumoured—see below, p. 157 footnote) 'the industry is in a relatively good shape to challenge its EEC competitors'. It is significant that, as against the 'good deal of nervousness' which it noted, *The Economist* only referred to these two giants as definitely sold on entering, and as helping to finance the lobbying necessary to achieve the desired political result.

Unlike the orthodox economists, Marxists unequivocally declare that the European Common Market is a direct emanation of monopoly capital at work, that it serves the interests of European capitalism's most powerful firms, and that whatever is said for propaganda purposes, it will never pursue a policy of equally standing up to the USA and the USSR for the simple reason that so much American capital is now involved in Europe that any basically anti-American policy is impossible except for an occasional gesture such as protests over President Nixon's import surtax, and non-co-operation with certain American proposals to solve the dollar problem. Even the recent 'dollar crisis' does not detract from US involvement in the ownership of capital in Europe.

Finally, as far as the European Common Market is concerned, it should not be forgotten that the Treaty of Rome is a guarantee to safeguard the capitalist system, so that the Market itself is dedicated to the perpetuation of production for private profit.

CHAPTER FIVE

Inequality of Income

Having considered the Labour Theory of Value and the source of Profit, it may appear somewhat incongruous to turn to the subject of inequality of incomes. However, it is necessary to deal with it, if only because of the widespread mythology which has grown up round Marxism, centring on the alleged role of 'equality' within the Marxist scheme of things.

If Marxist writings are closely studied, it will be found that nowhere is 'equality of income' considered either as an existing phenomenon or even as an objective. To Marxists, the trend of economic evolution is in the direction of an Age of Plenty in which 'each will contribute according to his ability and receive according to his needs'. We shall go into this more fully later, but it should be noted that nowhere is there an assumption that abilities and needs will ever be 'equal' as between persons.

If we are to search for a study of the economic effects of equalising incomes, we shall not get much help from Marxist writings, but shall find something in orthodox economics. Thus, Professor Pigou in his *Economics of Welfare* set out an argument in the 1920s, based on the application of the Law of Diminishing Marginal Utility to incomes themselves, in favour of greater equality of incomes in the interest of maximising welfare. He wrote: 'The old "law of diminishing utility" thus leads us securely to the proposition: Any cause which increases the absolute share of real income in the hands of the poor, provided that it does not lead to a contraction of the national dividend from any point of view, will, in general, increase economic welfare'.

(Pigou, op. cit., 4th ed., p. 89.) Note that there is here an important qualification, that such tendencies to equalise incomes must not in any way cause a reduction in the national dividend. In practice, political controversy centres on this proviso, since it is argued both that taxation of the rich lessens their capacity to save and invest, and that both higher income tax and free services to the relatively poor may lessen incentives to work. We shall return to this later.

However, ironical as it may seem, this theoretical argument for more equality comes from the orthodox school of economics, not from the Marxists. It may therefore be worth while to summarise the Marxist treatment of the subject, as differentiated from the rather unorthodox 'orthodox' treatment which it receives from Professor Pigou.

In expounding the Labour Theory of Value Marx assumes 'average labour' as a theoretical norm with which to work, rather as the orthodox economist, Alfred Marshall, postulated the 'representative firm'. But in practice Marx recognised that differences in the skill of labour had to be taken into account, as also the cost of education and training. Marx also recognised that certain specialised functions, such as superintendence, were a form of useful labour that would have to be paid for under any economic system. (See *supra*, p. 57.)

Again, various possibilities exist for differences in personal incomes from profits, according to movements in the market. So differences in incomes as such were accepted as inevitable by Marx. The distinction which he did make, as one which could be eliminated, was the difference between earned and unearned incomes, a difference which could not be eliminated under capitalism since this system depended on the perpetuation of private ownership of the means of production, and the income therefrom.

When Marx looked to the future, to a new communist (or socialist) economic order, he envisaged that wages would at first continue to be paid, and that they would not be equal. Thus, in *Capital* we find him, after dealing with the abstraction of a

'Robinson Crusoe', turning to 'a community of free individuals, carrying on their work with the means of production in common, in which the labour-power of all the different individuals is consciously applied as the combined labour-power of the community . . . social, instead of individual. . . . The total product of our community is a social product. One portion serves as fresh means of production and remains social. But another portion is consumed by the members as means of subsistence. A distribution of this portion among them is consequently necessary. The mode of this distribution will vary with the productive organisation of the community, and the degree of historical development attained by the producers'. (Op. cit., Vol. I, p. 90.)

A fuller discussion of this point is contained in the *Critique of the Gotha Programme*, which has become the main Marxist source book on this question. Here, on the use of such a term as 'equitable distribution', Marx commented that in a 'communist✗ society, as it *emerges* from capitalist society . . . the individual producer receives back from society—after the deductions have been made—exactly what he gives to it'. These deductions, says Marx, would have to provide 'cover for the replacement of the means of production used up,' 'additional portion for expansion of production,' 'reserve or insurance fund', 'the general costs of administration not belonging to production', a sum 'for the communal satisfaction of needs, such as schools, health services, etc.,' and 'funds for those unable to work.'

Only after the 'economic necessity' of making such deductions (which, with defence added, give a very accurate summary of what today happens in states with Marxist governments) is there left the sum that is to be divided among citizens as personal incomes. 'Accordingly the individual receives back from society— after the deductions have been made—exactly what he gives to it . . . The same amount of labour which he has given to society in one form, he receives back in another. . . . The right of the producers is *proportional* to the labour they supply; the equality consists in the fact that measurement is made with an *equal standard*, labour'. This labour must be measured by 'its duration or intensity. . . . It recognises no class differences, because everyone is only a worker like everyone else; but it tacitly recognises unequal individual endowment and thus productive capacity as natural privileges. *It is therefore a right of inequality in its content* . . . unequal individuals (and they would not be different individuals if they were not unequal) are only measurable by an equal standard in so far as they are brought under an equal point of view . . . in the present case are regarded *only as workers.* Further, one worker is married, another not; one has more children than another and so forth. Thus with an equal output, and hence an equal share in the social consumption fund, one will in fact receive more than another, one will be richer than another, and so on. . . .'

Hence also Lenin declared that 'the first phase of communism cannot produce justice and equality; differences, and unjust differences, in wealth will still exist, but the *exploitation* of man by man will have become impossible, because it will be impossible to seize the means of production'. (Lenin, *State and Revolution.*)

So when Stalin, whatever faults he was later blamed for, spent a part of his report to the 17th Communist Party Congress in 1939 condemning the view of some people 'that Socialism calls for equalisation', and stressed that Socialism (the first stage of Communism) meant 'the equal emancipation of all working people from exploitation . . . the equal abolition for all of private property in the means of production' and 'the equal duty of all to work according to their ability, and . . . to receive remuneration according to the amount of work performed', he was simply reaffirming the traditional views of Marx and Lenin. As to the future, he foresaw a '*Communist* society' when, based on abundance, all would 'receive remuneration according to their needs'.

This 'higher phase' was described by Marx in the *Gotha Programme* as one in which 'the enslaving subordination of individuals under division of labour' and also 'the antithesis between mental and physical labour' would have become things of the past; when labour would be 'not merely a means to live but . . . the prime necessity of life, after the productive forces have also increased with the all-round development of the individual, and all the springs of co-operative wealth flow more abundantly—only then can the narrow horizon of bourgeois right be fully left behind and society inscribe on its banners: "from each according to his ability, to each according to his needs" '.

It is clear from the above that Marxists take a long-term view of economic progress. Some critics may say that there is not much difference between such a long-term forecast and the traditional 'opium of the people' stigmatised as 'pie in the sky when you die'. But, at least, the Marxist perspective is rooted to earth, to be attained by collective human effort.

While it has always been the view of Marxists that, given public ownership of the means of production and their planned use for the benefit of the community, an equilibrium between resources and wants could be achieved, so that distribution according to need would ultimately become a reality; this very possibility has always been denied by the orthodox economists. And under capitalism this view is natural enough, for capitalism itself thrives on the creating of wants far beyond the point at which they arise spontaneously. Most of modern advertising is aimed at persuading people that they have unsatisfied wants. If, on the other hand, an economy is planned to satisfy human wants, and advertising is limited to informing people of what new products are available and no more, the tendency for wants to run ahead of resources can be held within bounds. In a society in which nobody is being hourly told that he or she has unsatisfied wants, that it is necessary to buy this or buy that in order to keep up with the Joneses or to ensnare the girl or boy down the road, then consumers' demand has a chance to settle at a reasonable level commensurate with society's capacity to produce.

Clearly, in all existing socialist countries today, a long period is still necessary to reach the sort of Age of Plenty which Marxists have always had in mind. Most of the socialist countries, for historical reasons by no means entirely economic, have come into existence in relatively underdeveloped areas in the intense austerity of wartime. They have had to overcome economic backwardness compared with the advanced capitalist countries, in Stalin's words, 'to catch up and surpass'. In any case, in any country whatsoever, a long process is necessary for a transition from the capitalist system to the sort of Age of Plenty envisaged.

If we take 'socialism' to denote the public ownership of the means of production; together with a national economic Plan for their optimum utilisation in the present and future interests of the community, then the countries under Marxist leadership today may all be called 'socialist'. In this sense the term is used to denote what Marx always referred to as the 'first phase' of Communism.

In all such countries, it must be recognised, planning is not perfect, but is liable to human error just as private enterprise is. There are possibilities of over-estimates and under-estimates and bottlenecks, as well as the successful carrying out of plans.

In such a system, payment is made according to work done. But how is the value of work done assessed? In Marxist theory, it ought to be assessed by what is socially necessary to produce it. This does not only involve standards of *living*, but standards of *training, qualifications* and *responsibility*. In fact, within socialist society, Supply and Demand do here play a limited role. For short of *directed* labour—which *did* exist in the USSR during and just after the last war—free labour has got to be *attracted* to the jobs which are considered most socially necessary at any time. When, therefore, a socialist government finds it necessary to attract more people to the teaching profession, or to coal mining, or to pioneering work in an undeveloped area, it offers higher pay for the work: in other words, in a situation where any kind of work has become socially more necessary, society is ready to pay more for it. This is, under socialism and given the free movement of labour, the only way apart from propaganda which the government can use to attract labour where is it socially most necessary.

On the other hand, when a job nears completion, as is bound to occur under Socialism as also under capitalism, the Socialist government is able to plan in advance, workers are warned in good time, and ample provision can be made for them to move to similar work in other places, or to re-train for other work according to their inclination. In the 1930s, when the first line of the Moscow Metro was nearing completion, several thousand workers who had gained experience in underground tunnelling techniques became redundant owing to the fact that far more mechanised techniques had been adopted for use on further lines. This was known in good time, and the Central Council of Trade Unions was asked to help in distributing the workers to jobs for which they were qualified. As a result, the several thousand workers were dispersed—at public expense—to various parts of the country where their tunnelling experience could be utilised.

While the distribution of labour naturally raises its own specific problems under socialist planning, the subject of equalisation of incomes does not arise. Differences will vary from time to time, according to the changes in social needs and customs.

Since the death of Stalin in the USSR there have been a number of measures aimed at reducing the gap between the highest and lowest earnings. At the same time there has been a steady advance in free social services from which the lowest income-groups gain the most. The policy has now been adopted in the USSR, for application from 1974 onwards, of paying a state allowance to every family where income *per head* is less than 50 roubles per month. The sum itself is not important, but the principle, that every citizen from birth should be guaranteed a minimum income, is one more clear step in the direction of distribution according to need.

Let us now return to the camp of the orthodox economists. The question of economic inequality under capitalism has been considered by a number of individuals, of whom Professor Pigou was the leading example in the 1920s, while Professor R. H. Tawney, in his *Acquisitive Society*, was rather more critical of capitalism as such and less highly regarded among the orthodox economists. In recent years Professor Titmuss has done much research into the distribution of real wealth and income among the population and has somewhat deflated the image of the welfare state by showing to what an extent the benefits have been, in effect, provided by the taxing of those who most benefited.

We may now pursue a little further Professor Pigou's theory that welfare may benefit from a tendency to equalise incomes. His reasoning was simple enough: Of two men, one on £10,000 a year and one on £1,000 a year, the satisfaction received from the last pound of the former (£1 in £10,000) is likely to be less than the satisfaction received from the last pound of the latter (£1 in £1,000). This is strictly in accord with the accepted Law of Diminishing Marginal Utility of orthodox economics, though several orthodox economists have challenged Professor Pigou's view on this, maintaining that nobody can assess the satisfaction obtained from income. However, individual psychology is probably sufficiently homogeneous to justify Pigou's reasoning.

It follows that in society as a whole, a transfer of income from the richer to the poorer will increase total satisfaction, since the rich man's loss is less than the poor man's gain. This principle is operated, within strict limits, in the British form of progressively graduated income tax.

But there are several other matters to be taken into account. Professor Pigou himself would not press a policy of equalising incomes beyond the point at which it would have adverse effects on production. And there is undoubtedly something to be said for the view that taxes on incomes may curb saving and investment, and thus the private supply of capital; and that it may curb readiness to work, if too much of extra earnings is to be 'taken by the government'. Therefore there is a theoretical limit to equalisation of income under capitalism, the point at which any increase in welfare through redistribution is offset by an equal and opposite decline in production—the source of all welfare. As these limits are in practice incalculable, they throw open a limitless area for discussion and political polemic.

At this point it is useful to turn back to what happens under socialism, in the country which was the first in history to attempt to apply Marxist principles, the USSR. For in the USSR it is precisely to provide an incentive to labour that wages and salaries are graduated. Moreover, other incomes are practically non-existent, so that we have to do with an economy in which income means income from work. It will be noted that private saving here is a negligible source of capital, and therefore no question arises about inequality of incomes being necessary to provide saving and capital. On the other hand, however, people are paid according to the skill and responsibility of their work as currently assessed by the planning authorities, the employing organisations and the trade unions.*

D. Lane, in a recent book on the USSR (*Politics and Society in the USSR*, 1970) has collected, mainly from American sources, several assessments of the distribution of incomes in the USSR. Lenski, for example, is quoted as saying that in the USSR the maximum incomes are only 300 times the minimum, and only 100 times the average, as against 11,000 times and 7,000 times respectively in the USA. And Lane himself points out that the magnitude of 'individual *unearned* income' in the capitalist states is the main reason why 'income differentiation in Soviet society is certainly less'. And while Lane considers that 'social inequality is a universal social phenomenon' (which Marx would probably have agreed with, so long as *class* inequality was excluded) he finds in the USSR 'no property-owning class'. Large-scale industries, therefore, can function without the *private* accumulation of property and the inequalities to which it gives rise. . . The main dispute in the USSR has never been over the ratio between the richest and the poorest and in practice this ratio is now very much lower than in western societies.' (Lane, op. cit., pp. 403, 416f.)

* It should not be assumed that, in the socialist countries, the only incentives are material. Moral or political incentives also exist, such as state encouragement to enter certain jobs, and honours and decorations for outstanding work. There is also considerable variation between the countries with Marxist governments as to the extent to which material and moral incentives are to be stressed at any time. In the USSR wage-differentials by geographical region are used as well as propaganda to encourage workers to move where they are most needed.

Given the public ownership of the means of production, and the public responsibility to provide for an expansion of capital, the 'need' for the rich, as providers of capital, falls to the ground. In replacing a system of private capital investment by planned public investment, Marxist states do away with the need for high incomes as a source of capital. In the Soviet state budget for 1972 allocations to the national economy (i.e. public investment) amounted to 82,600 million roubles out of a total state expenditure of 165,100 million. As against these figures social and cultural measures took 62,900 and defence 17,900 million roubles. So investment in the economy took just over half the year's state expenditure. Of the revenue, 90.8 per cent came from the economy, and taxes on citizens were not more than 15,000 thousand million, or 8.6 per cent of the total revenue. Hence private saving and investment, the basis of capitalism, are now nearly negligible in the USSR; and even private taxes are withering away.

It is clear that in the USSR and other socialist countries the governments have simply to adjust earnings so as to ensure that everyone, by work, makes the optimum contribution to production. At the same time, by continuously expanding free social services, health, education, pensions and subsidised housing, together with family allowances, the provision of services according to need is constantly expanding. Obviously the provision of universally free services, and ultimately universally free goods, cannot be achieved overnight, but progress towards this goal has been continuing ever since the First Five-Year Plan was launched in 1928.

When socially planned production reaches such a state of abundance that it can really be described as an Age of Plenty, and when education and social habits have reached a level at which life is only worth while to the individual if it entails useful work for society, at that point it can be said that 'each will contribute according to his ability and receive according to his needs.'

F

CHAPTER SIX

Competition and Monopoly

Capitalism is referred to as the 'free enterprise' system or 'competitive capitalism' on the part of the orthodox school, whereas Marxist economists repeatedly refer to 'monopoly capitalism' or 'state monopoly capitalism' in order to describe its present phase. If orthodox economists are confronted with the proposition that competitive capitalism must, by its very nature, lead towards monopoly, they find themselves in difficulties, since most orthodox economists, with the exception of Schumpeter, have never studied the nature of competitive capitalism sufficiently dynamically to perceive that it must lead to its own destruction.

In orthodox economics it is today recognised that any branch of the capitalist economic system may range between the two postulated extremes of 'perfect competition' and 'complete monopoly'. In the first case it is assumed that there are so many firms of much of a muchness in size that no one of them can affect market price. As in practice such conditions are increasingly not realised, the state of perfect competition is increasingly admitted to be a theoretical abstraction, and 'imperfect competition' is now taken to be the norm.

At the other end of the scale is monopoly which, in theory, means one supplier only in the market. Here again it is realised that this is an abstraction and the British Monopolies Commission took as its criterion the supply of as much as one-third of a market by a single firm as sufficient justification for qualifying as a suspect in regard to monopolistic practices.

Basically, the difference is this: under free competition each firm produces up to the point at which price just covers marginal costs. It is assumed, therefore, that on this basis everyone produces as much as possible at the lowest possible price at his scale of production. Under monopoly, however, since the supplier has no rivals in the market, he can restrict supply and (if the demand for his commodity is inelastic) his total revenue from sales will increase. Hence there is a likelihood that many monopolies will restrict supply deliberately, thus keeping up prices, which is not in the interests of the community as consumers. It follows from this that, so long as competition prevails, consumers may be said to be 'sovereign' in the sense that, by offering a higher price they can cause more to be produced and *vice versa*. But if a monopoly exists this is not necessarily so. In this case a rise in demand price may not call forth any extra supply, the supplier may simply choose to gain from the greater demand by charging higher prices. Under modern conditions, so many sources of supply are partly monopolised that it is quite impossible to assume 'consumers' sovereignty', though even under competitive capitalism the power of the consumer was undoubtedly exaggerated.

Professor Galbraith goes so far as to assert that 'in the assumption that power belongs as a matter of course to capital, all economists are Marxians' nowadays (*New Industrial State*, p. 49). This is certainly an exaggeration, because in both American and British economics textbooks the doctrine of 'consumers' sovereignty' is still frequently taught, which is a natural result of a system which starts out with 'perfect competition' as its initial assumption.

In the contemporary orthodox landscape, monopoly is still treated as some sort of exceptional fringe phenomenon which, when it occurs, has to be specially dealt with. The Anti-Trust legislation in the USA at the end of the last century and the British Monopolies Commission since 1946 are cited as examples of the curbing of anti-social monopolistic activity. And while 'imperfect competition' is now admitted to be the general rule, all the arguments based on a non-existent 'perfect competition' are still used in defence of a system called 'competitive capitalism'.

On the other hand, when an economist gets down to studying the British Monopolies Commission at work, we are given a picture of anything but effectiveness. For example, in his *Guide to the British Economy* (1965), Peter Donaldson studies the work of the Monopolies Commission and comments that 'as an instrument for controlling restrictive practices in industry the Commission must be judged an almost total failure. Its progress was agonisingly slow'. Between 1948 and 1956 'it had investigated only twenty-one cases'. Its membership was small, ten, later raised to twenty-three. It had to examine each case separately and 'its conclusions and recommendations were limited to that industry alone.' It had a very limited budget. It 'singularly failed to provide industry with any self-rectifying incentive. There was no tendency . . . for the mere threat of investigation to induce British manufacturers to put their houses in order . . . and one of the most damning criticisms of the Commission's activities was the failure to arouse any real public interest'. Also, 'the Board of Trade which was responsible for selecting the subjects of the Commission's enquiries . . . showed a somewhat staggering lack of imagination in choosing'. Again, it was a government department that was responsible for enforcement, and though 'the Commission found practices contrary to the public interest in all but three of its investigations, in only one case was an order for the abandonment made'. Donaldson comments: 'Cynics might argue that this was precisely what had been intended—to make a nominal show of controlling big business without going to the extreme of making such control effective.' (Donaldson, op. cit., pp. 88–90.) Marxists would naturally be among the 'cynics'.

Donaldson's comments were published in 1965, but more recently *The Economist* (6 November 1971) has echoed the same sentiments. 'At present,' it wrote, 'there are only a dozen men inside the Department of Trade and Industry who keep an eye on anti-monopoly policy. The Monopolies Commission takes up to five years, when it chooses, to complete its enquiries. In this drowsy atmosphere, industry can and does get away with competitive murder.'

To Marx, monopoly was the natural end-product of successful competition, arising inevitably out of the accumulation and concentration of capital. 'The battle of competition is fought by cheapening of commodities. The cheapening of commodities depends, *ceteris paribus*, on the productiveness of labour, and this again on the scale of production. Therefore, the larger capitals beat the smaller.' There is also, 'with the development of the capitalist mode of production . . . an increase in the minimum amount of individual capital necessary to carry on a business under its normal conditions. The smaller capitals, therefore, crowd into spheres of production which Modern Industry has only sporadically or incompletely got hold of. Here competition rages . . . It always ends in the ruin of many small capitalists, whose capitals partly pass into the hands of their conquerors, partly vanish.' (*Capital*, Vol. I, pp. 686 *et seq.*)

Striking confirmation of this analysis by Marx is to be found in figures published by the Monopolies Commission in 1969 in its *General Observations on Mergers*. A survey of British manufacturing companies between 1961 and 1968, covering all companies with net assets of more than £500,000, showed that the total number of these companies had declined from 1312 to 908 between the beginning of 1961 and the end of 1968. By this latter date the 28 largest companies held 50 per cent of the total net assets of the 908, while the 908 companies together were calculated as holding not less than 80 per cent of the total net assets of all the manufacturing companies in the United Kingdom.

Apart from the above tendency, Marx noted that 'with capitalist production an altogether new force comes into play—the credit system' which 'draws by invisible threads the money resources scattered all over the surface of society into the hands of individual or associated capitalists . . . and finally it transforms itself into an immense social mechanism for the centralisation of capitals'. (*Capital*, loc. cit.) This tendency is illustrated in Britain today by a new type of merger, the 'conglomerate', which brings together under one umbrella completely different branches of economic activity. There is no common interest in production whatsoever, financial reasons only dictate the 'marriages'. Robert Heller in the *Business Observer* of 11 November 1971, gave some outstanding examples: The Hanson Trust, producing a range from colour printing to submersible pumps; Ralli International, from timber to jute; First National Finance, from hire purchase to publishing; Barclay Securities, 'toys, drugs and posters'; and the Triumph Investment Trust, 'insurance to scrap metal'.

Marx goes on: 'Competition and credit, the two most powerful levers of centralisation, develop in proportion as capitalist production and accumulation do. At the same time the progress of accumulation' gives rise to 'those gigantic industrial enterprises, which depend for their realisation on a previous centralisation of capitals. Centralisation in a certain line of industry would have reached its extreme limit, if all the individual capitals invested in it would have been amalgamated into one single capital'. (Ibid.)

To these remarks of Marx we, in the 1970s, may add a reference to the current wave of mergers and take-overs as simply a continuation of the process pinpointed by Marx, now not only in 'certain lines' but uniting completely different lines so that a 'practical monopoly' may develop covering a number of different products simultaneously, the degree of monopoly varying with each particular commodity.

While Marx saw clearly the in-built tendency for *successful* competition to lead inevitably in the direction of monopoly, and in this he was years ahead of his contemporaries and even of our own contemporary orthodox economists, his whole analysis of value, surplus value and price was rooted in the then existing competitive capitalism. He therefore assumed that market conditions would tend to force prices down in the direction of costs, and that profits would tend to equalise between capitalists. Baran and Sweezy therefore have a point when they say that today 'we cannot be content with patching up the competitive model which underlies' Marx's theory, because 'the typical economic unit in the capitalist world is not the small firm . . . but a large-scale enterprise producing a significant share of the output of an industry . . . The typical economic unit, in other words, has the

attributes which we once thought to be possessed only by monopolies' (Baran and Sweezy, *Monopoly Capital*, p. 6). Similarly,
and a parallel point, Marx in his day noted, but did not develop,
the contradiction between developed capitalism and the conse-
quent underdevelopment of much of the rest of the world.

Baran, in his *Political Economy of Growth*, follows up this
line of thought by pointing out that nowadays Marx's 'mechanism of the equalisation of the rates of profit operates only in the
greatly compressed competitive sector of the economic system.
There the rates of profit are low and the mass of profits available
for investment relatively small'. But 'in the monopolistic and
oligolopolistic sphere of the economy the rates of profit on invested capital are unequal but predominantly high and the mass
of profit available for investment prodigiously large'. (Op. cit.,
p. 85.) Our example from Fords on p. 47 is such a case.

Baran points out that an effect of this tendency is the piling up
of reserves which the big near-monopolistic firms 'find . . . unprofitable to plough . . . back into their own enterprises and
increasingly difficult to invest . . . elsewhere . . . There is consequently a tendency towards underemployment and stagnation, a
tendency that was precisely identified by Marx a hundred years
ago.' (Ibid.)

Now, just as production becomes monopolised and we move
further and further away from purely competitive conditions, so
profits and all surplus-value are augmented by the profits arising
from monopolistic sales policies. It thus so happens that while
Marx's falling rate of profit may well be operating at the point of
production, large firms can more than offset this by raising prices
above value at the point of sale. If this occurs widely in a community, we would expect a general tendency for prices to rise,
rather than the earlier tendency for competition to keep prices
down. The general inflationary trend in capitalist countries since
1946 may to a great extent be explained by this: Workers'
organisations have made exploitation at the point of production
more difficult, especially during a period of relatively full employment. Therefore all those employers who today enjoy

near-monopolistic influence on prices have recouped themselves for having to pay higher wages by raising prices.

Emile Burns (Op. cit., pp. 44–5) gives a clear example of this. 'The practice of raising prices so that they bring in more than the capitalists lose from a wage or tax increase is so widespread that it has become a settled policy. In the House of Commons on 11 March 1964, Mr James Callaghan, then in Opposition, gave instances of the proportion of wages to total costs in various sections of engineering. In general engineering the proportion was 33 per cent; in motor vehicles, 16 per cent. But, he said, following on a recent 5 per cent rise in engineering wages, employers had raised the prices of engineering products by 4 to 8 per cent, thus making big increases in profits on the pretext of the higher wages they had to pay.'

In addition, so long as the State itself is capitalist, the State can, through its taxation policy, favour profits at the expense of real wages. Burns gives an example. 'The shifting of the main burden of taxation from the capitalists to the workers is shown by the fact that the total income of companies rose between 1951 and 1963 by £2,776 million, or 88 per cent, while the direct taxation on them rose by only £173 million, or 12 per cent.

'In the same period indirect taxes on the people (what the official statistics describe as 'taxes on expenditure') rose from £2,274 million in 1951 to £4,048 million in 1963, an increase of £1,774 million—ten times the amount of the increased taxation that fell on companies.' (Burns, ibid.)

Since in 1970 a government came to power in Britain which undisguisedly represented the interests of big business, we have seen unemployment rise to the highest figure since 1946, tax relief for incomes which has put additional thousands of pounds per annum into the pockets of the top directors of industry, and the Civil List and incomes of M.P.s and Ministers raised very substantially while a strict 'incomes policy' is still being advocated for the majority. At the same time there is a boom in stocks and shares. These facts all illustrate the working of a state which is essentially defending the interests of monopoly capital.

The history of expansion is different for different companies. If, for example, we take Unilever Ltd, we find a continuous process of growth which has been a logical expansion from the humble producers of one product, margarine. This demanded the acquisition of control of sources of raw materials, and this led to expansion both into the sources of palm oil in Africa and whale blubber on the high seas. These raw materials in turn were put to more and more different uses. By buying up companies and absorbing lines of production using the same basic raw materials, Unilever has grown to an international giant whose products range from the original margarine to cosmetics, sausages and ice-cream (produced, of course, under many different trade names).

Again, while orthodox economists have tended to isolate, and treat separately, the subjects of competition on the one hand (considered in the department labelled 'Theory of Value') and of the growth of firms on the other (treated under 'scale' in the 'Production' department), Marx from the outset saw the essential unity of the two: 'Under competition, the increase in the minimum of capital required for the successful operation of an independent industrial establishment in keeping with the increase in productivity assumes the following aspect: As soon as the new and more expensive equipment has become universally established, smaller capitals are henceforth excluded from these enterprises. . . .

'We have seen that the growing accumulation of capital implies its growing concentration. Thus the power of capital . . . grows over the heads of the real producers. Capital shows itself more and more as a social power, whose agent the capitalist is . . . Capital becomes a strange, independent, social power, which stands opposed to society.' (*Capital*, Vol. III, pp. 308–10.)

Since the death of Marx, the international ramifications of capital have enormously increased. Lenin, in his *Imperialism*, used the findings of the English economist, J. A. Hobson, who, he wrote, 'gives an excellent and comprehensive description of the principal economic and political characteristics of imperialism'.

'Fifty years ago,' wrote Lenin in 1920 in this work, 'when Marx was writing *Capital*, free competition appeared to most economists to be a "natural law". The official scientists tried, by a conspiracy of silence, to kill the works of Marx, which by a theoretical and historical analysis of capitalism showed that free competition gives rise to the concentration of production, which, in turn, at a certain stage of development, leads to monopoly. Today monopoly has become a fact. The economists are writing mountains of books in which they describe the diverse manifestations of monopoly, and continue to declare in chorus that "Marxism is refuted".' (Op. cit., Moscow, 1934, p. 20.)

Lenin described imperialism as being, in essence, 'monopoly capitalism'. And he summarised its principle characteristics as being that (1) it arose 'out of the concentration of production at a very advanced stage of development'. (2) 'Monopolies have accelerated the seizure of the most important sources of raw materials'. (3) 'Monopoly has sprung from the banks' which 'have developed from modest intermediary enterprises into the monopolists of finance capital. Some three or five of the biggest banks in each of the foremost capitalist countries have achieved the "personal union" of industrial and banking capital, and concentrated in their hands the disposal of thousands upon thousands of millions which form the greater part of the capital and revenue of entire countries.' (4) 'Monopoly has grown out of colonial policy. To the numerous "old" motives of colonial policy, finance capital has added the struggle for the sources of raw materials, for the export of capital, for "spheres of influence", i.e., for spheres of good business, concessions, monopolist profits and so on; in fine, for economic territory in general.'

Three comments should be made on this passage in the 1970s:

First, it has often been said that Lenin's emphasis on the role of the banks, while true of Germany, was not true in the case of Britain. But in *The Economist* of 18 September 1971 we read a feature article on the possibility that by 1980 Britain will be 'a bank-dominated rather than stock-market-orientated economy.' And the article continues: 'In Germany and Japan it is common for big firms to be 70 per cent bank-financed and 30 per cent stock-market-financed, while in Britain and America the patterns are likely to be rather the other way round.

'In consequence, commercial bankers in Germany and Japan have much more power over individual companies—and especially over actions by individual companies with inefficient boards of directors—than bankers have here.' But 'it seems a reasonable forecast that in ten years' time some bodies called banks . . . will be financing a much larger part of, and be much more heavily influencing the boards of directors of, some great British companies than is at all usual today.'

As with Marx, Lenin's words are being proved prophetic.

Secondly, a comment of Lord Balogh is worth quoting on the Bretton Woods Conference of 1944, which set up the International Monetary Fund, which he describes as having 'established the eventual supremacy of money-capital in the West.' (Balogh, op. cit., p. 135.) It is also interesting to note, by the way, that it is extremely rare—if it ever happens at all—for an economics textbook to point out that the *International* Monetary Fund is under effective *American* financial control.

Thirdly, attention should be paid to Lenin's use of the term 'economic' territories, since those words today have a far greater significance, owing to the growth of the number of politically independent countries, than they had when they were written. Many of the countries that now fly their own flags, but which were colonies before 1945, are still in varying degrees the victims of the vagaries of foreign capital. So much is this so, that the late President Kwame Nkrumah of Ghana described this in his book, *Neo-Colonialism,* as the 'worst form of imperialism.'

'The struggle against neo-colonialism is not aimed at excluding the capital of the developed world from operating in less developed countries,' he wrote, but 'at preventing the financial power of the developed countries being used in such a way as to impoverish the less developed . . . A State in the grip of neo-colonialism is not master of its own destiny.' (Nkrumah, op. cit., pp. x, xi.) And the book contains a number of examples of monopolistic companies in the West, often entwined together by means of interlocking directorates, which are making enormous profits out of Africa. Examples are given such as Liberia where 'two-fifths of Liberia's total income accrues to foreign firms (*UN Report E/CN.* 14/246, 7 January 1964)'. (Ibid., p. 237.) The fate of Ghana itself, after the military coup in 1966, has been the subordination of an ever greater proportion of its own resources and capital investment to the control of foreign companies. Again, an analysis of the development of world trade since 1946 has shown a steadily deteriorating situation for all the underdeveloped countries in their terms of trade with the developed ones. So that, whatever may be the monetary picture of 'aid', the underdeveloped countries have continuously had to pay higher prices for their imports of industrial goods in terms of their traditional exports.

So when Marx wrote of capital as becoming a 'strange, independent, social power, which stands opposed to society,' he was indeed forecasting the present world-wide situation. Smaller and newly-independent countries have had to contend with the operation on their territories of vast international concerns whose total assets and incomes far exceed the total resources and revenues of the governments of many of the countries in which they operate. Barclays Bank DCO, with its £500 million of capital, operates all over Africa in countries many of whose 'independent' governments cannot lay hands on a fraction of such a sum. Even in advanced Britain, decisions can be made by a board of directors in the USA whether to invest or not to invest in a new enterprise. And a recent report on the state of foreign investment in Canada 'sounded the now familiar warning about the dangers to Canada from having so much of its industry controlled from abroad, principally from the United States. Among other things, the Canadian government is hampered in its efforts to run a full-employment policy if key decisions affecting Canadian subsidiaries are taken abroad and motivated by concern for the parent's global interests.

'These are precisely the same sort of doubts about the impact of the multinationals voiced all over the world in present years: what is special about Canada is the abnormally high proportion of its industry that is controlled by them.' (*The Economist*, 27 November 1971.)

Many capitalist countries, in their overseas development in the epoch of imperialism and neo-colonialism, have been enabled to make large super-profits by the exploitation of colonial labour. In so far as they have done this, they have found a way of offsetting on their home territory the tendency for the rate of profit to fall.

But it would be wrong to assume that there is not a resistance to such developments in the countries which suffer from them. Egypt, which while politically independent was for many years economically in a 'neo-colonial' position (to use the modern term), finally nationalised the Suez Canal, and followed this by a number of measures to defend itself against foreign exploitation. Other African countries have taken measures to nationalise (at least to the extent of 51 per cent) foreign-owned enterprises, including banks. Libya in regard to its oil, Zambia in regard to copper, Uganda and Tanzania can all be quoted as examples. In Latin America also the same process is taking place.

It follows naturally that the countries in which most is being done to develop the economy independently of imperialism gravitate for aid towards the Marxist-led countries. For the socialist governments are prepared to advance capital on totally different terms from those traditional under imperialism. Whereas capitalist 'investment' gives ownership rights in perpetuity, the supply of capital by the socialist countries always takes the form of long-term credit at low rates of interest (2 to $2\frac{1}{2}$ per cent as a rule). The capital sum is repayable over 12 to 15 years, in the form of the traditional exports of the countries concerned. Any capital equipment purchased by the underdeveloped country is, from the time of purchase, the property of the country concerned. It is therefore clear that the practice of the socialist countries in supplying capital equipment to underdeveloped countries is a complete break with capitalist and imperialist traditional type of investment, though there is no doubt since

1946 that it has had some influence on the developed countries themselves in the terms on which they now supply capital.

With the process of economic growth of firms, and the resultant increase in imperfect competition tending towards monopoly, the orthodox economists have taken note of these changes up to a point. But since their whole theoretical approach is still rooted in the competitive *assumption*, they have never liberated themselves from the view that monopoly is in some way abnormal. As a result, many words are spent on 'how to control' monopoly, and very little is said about the converting of private monopoly into public property, or of the primary responsibility of monopoly for rising prices. (See *Postscript* to this chapter.)

One economist of recent years, J. K. Galbraith, has attempted a revision of the orthodox theory of profit-maximisation as the motive force of capitalism. He has drawn attention to the way in which, in the modern large joint stock company, ownership by the ordinary shareholders has become increasingly divorced from enterprise and management, now the function of salaried personnel. This, suggests Galbraith, is a new feature in capitalism. He portrays the organisers of enterprise in this new set-up as being motivated, not by the desire for profit, but by the desire for success, of achieving the status that goes with the management of a successful enterprise. In such a situation, directors are concerned with company-building as their main aim, and 'so long as earnings are above a certain minimum, it would be widely agreed that the management has little to fear from the shareholders'. (Galbraith, op. cit., p. 115.)

Galbraith's directors of corporations, in re-investing as capital part of the profits of their corporations rather than pay more than necessary of their surplus-value in dividends, are simply conforming to Marx's pattern of capitalist behaviour. For to Marx's capitalist it was not 'values in use and the enjoyment of them, but exchange-value and its augmentation, that spur him into action . . . he ruthlessly forces the human race to produce for production's sake; he thus forces the development of the productive powers of society'. In this context 'his own private consumption is a robbery perpetrated on accumulation . . . To accumulate, is to conquer the world of social wealth, to increase the mass of human beings exploited by him, and thus to extend both the direct and indirect sway of the capitalist.' (*Capital*, Vol. I, p. 649.)

When therefore directors of modern companies behave in the way outlined by Galbraith, this is nothing new to capitalism, and in fact the shareholders, who own the capital, are satisfied enough with limited dividends so long as there is a surplus to be ploughed back into the business. Their current income may suffer, but their accumulation of wealth gains. The difference between today and yesterday in this connection lies in size of enterprise and the specialisation which has developed between the owners of capital (shareholders) and those who exercise the entrepreneur function in practice (the salaried directors and managers).

The fact that 1971 has seen unemployment in Britain reach the million mark for the first time since 1946, while capital investment *abroad* approaches a record total, rubs home the point of the internationalisation of capital. Investment of British capital abroad amounted to £667 million in 1969, £730 million in 1970, and according to Treasury returns reached £663 million in the first six months of 1971. The difficulty which British owners of capital find in investment at a profit in their own industries also throws light on the tendency for more and more firms to coalesce for financial reasons, though they have little if anything in common from the point of view of production. (See above, p. 78.)

Marx's view is well summed up in the words: 'The development of capitalist production makes it constantly necessary to keep increasing the amount of the capital laid out in a given industrial undertaking, and competition makes the immanent laws of capitalist production to be felt by each individual capitalist as external coercive laws. It compels him to keep constantly extending his capital, in order to preserve it, but extend it he cannot, except by means of progressive accumulation . . . he thus forces the development of the productive powers of society, and creates the material conditions which alone can form the basis of a higher form of society, a society in which the full and free development of every individual forms its ruling principle.' (*Capital*, Vol. I, p. 649.)

Hence to Marxists, competitive capitalism of necessity leads to monopoly capitalism, for all its material progress. And the contradictions in monopoly capitalism, despite the vast resources now available to humanity, are so great that their full potentialities can only be exploited if private monopoly is replaced by publicly owned monopolies run in the public interest. This would mean policies, of course, of passing on to the consumer, in the form of lower prices or lower taxes, the benefits from all increases in the productivity of labour.

Postscript

When this book was already in proof, an article was received from the Soviet Marxist publication *World Economy & International Relations* (No. 5, 1972) on the subject of the current inflation in the capitalist world. In a well-reasoned article, the author, R. Entov, makes a similar point to that which is made in this book. He notes that, despite all the theories of the orthodox economists of capitalism, 'in reality the development of inflation is now organically connected with the domination of monopolistic forms of economic relations . . . The futility of all attempts to curb the inflationary rise of prices once again demonstrates that the roots of the process extend deeply into the structure of the modern capitalist economy. Inflation is a kind of chronic disease of state-monopoly capitalism'.

CHAPTER SEVEN

'Can we beat Karl Marx?'

Ever since its days as *The Manchester Guardian*, *The Guardian* has been regarded as a serious English daily newspaper read widely by economists. It is one of the few serious newspapers, and therefore the headline 'Can we beat Karl Marx?' which appeared not so long ago (9 November 1970) above one of its leading articles must not be taken as frivolous. The article dealt with the problems of inflation. Five months later *The Economist*, perhaps the most serious of London's weeklies, headed a feature with the words 'Unemployment, on, on, up and up'. And this article opened with the phrase: 'Unemployment in Britain is now higher than at any time since 1940.' (Loc. cit., 24 April 1971.)

These two articles, taken together, epitomised the basic problems facing Britain's economy at the outset of the 1970s. And not only in regard to Britain, for in an OEDC report on 'Inflation: The Present Problem' (December 1970) we read that 'there is no single or simple panacea for inflation' and that there are areas 'where unemployment is rising towards unacceptable levels'.

When *The Guardian* asked its rhetorical question about Marx: 'Are we, then, doomed to provide Karl Marx with posthumous proof of his theories?' the editorial answer, predictably, was 'no'.

But this answer was so demonstratively ignorant of Marx's expressed views that the assertion that he 'has been proved wrong on fundamentals' simply did not hold water. 'The workers,' said *The Guardian*, 'far from being denied a fair share of profits and so becoming poorer, are vastly better off'.

G

Now, first of all, Marx never at any time wrote of workers receiving a 'fair', or even an 'unfair', 'share of profits'. For the very essence of his approach was the profits as such, and all other surplus-value, were the result of exploitation, an 'unfair' process by which the workers were deprived of part of their contribution to production.

Secondly, Marx did not deny that, with the development of technology, the workers could become better off out of what *The Guardian* calls 'the proceeds of prosperity' or what Marx would have called the 'greater productiveness of labour'.

In the *Communist Manifesto*, it is true, Marx and Engels did write that the 'modern labourer, instead of rising with the progress of industry, sinks deeper and deeper below the conditions of existence of his own class. He becomes a pauper, and pauperism develops more rapidly than population and wealth.' The same point is made once in *Capital* (Vol. I, pp. 708–9). Nevertheless, Marx stressed the existence of a struggle to resist such a tendency.

At other points, moreover, Marx pointed to the existence of counter-tendencies, as already quoted (*supra*, p. 33, *Capital*, Vol. I, p. 573) to the effect that 'it is possible with an increasing productiveness of labour, for the price of labour-power to keep on falling, and yet this fall to be accompanied by a constant growth in the mass of the labourer's means of subsistence', though Marx does add that the gap between the labourer's position and that of the capitalist would keep on widening. Again, in *Wage-labour and Capital*, he wrote that a 'rapid growth of productive capital brings about an equally rapid growth of wealth, luxury, social needs, social enjoyments. Thus, although the enjoyments of the worker have risen, the social satisfaction that they give has fallen in comparison with the increased enjoyments of the capitalists'. It is clear that, in the light of these statements, Marx was very far from denying the possibility of what are now called the 'welfare state' and 'affluence', though what he did not envisage was the length of the duration of capitalism in which such conditions might mature. Moreover, implicit in his writing throughout is the struggle of the workers against exploitation, so that against the tendency to depress their standards there is a constant struggle to resist.

For a contemporary Marxist view on this question we may refer to the article of Willi Garns in *World Marxist Review* (no. 3, 1970) mentioned earlier, in which he wrote: 'In the post-war period the living standards of the working people in the industrial capitalist countries, . . . their real wages and the social benefits they enjoy, have gone up to a certain extent. This is due to the rapid growth of the productive forces and a change in the pattern of skills, but above all to the strengthening of the positions of the working class in the social struggle as a result of the com-petition between the socialist and capitalist systems', this latter being a point which Marx could not have foreseen. Garns also noted that 'State monopoly regulation and the scientific and technological revolution undoubtedly account for the fact that industrial production in the leading capitalist countries today is growing faster than before.' These words were printed in 1970. Subsequently they read rather optimistically for capitalism.

While *The Guardian*, in the article with whose headline and quotation we opened this chapter, prescribed only one possible solution, 'a return to economic growth'; it sharply rejected a 'wage freeze' or a 'Prices and Incomes Policy', because 'prices and dividends, no less than wages and salaries, would have to come under control.' But *The Economist*, five months later, blamed the rising unemployment on the workers alone: 'The current roaring wage inflation has bitten sharply into profits and forced employers to cut down their labour forces. . . The situation has been aggravated by the pitifully small rate of economic growth.'

Hence two publications, both spokesmen of capitalism, dis-agree. To *The Guardian*, economic growth is the solution. To *The Economist*, wages are primarily to blame while the slow growth rate is merely an aggravation. These different views are typical of the sort of range of opinion and controversy which are acceptable within the framework of orthodox economics. *The*

Economist's reasoning, though not intentionally, confirms Marx's contention that there is a constant struggle between labour and capital, and that the capitalist must inevitably desire a reserve army of labour as a means of keeping down wages.

Up to the time of the world economic crisis of 1929–30, orthodox economists regarded the 'trade cycle', 'business cycle', 'industrial cycle', 'industrial fluctuations' as an endemic feature of the economic system. Endless books were written speculating on its causes, ranging from the 'sun spot' theory of Jevons, according to which fluctuations in the strength of the sun's rays led to fluctuations in the world's harvests, causing fluctuations in agricultural prices which affected the entire economies of the world; to the much more sophisticated works of such economists as Schumpeter, Beveridge, Pigou and Keynes, which recognised the complexity of the problem, denied any single overriding cause, and tended to favour public spending to replace private spending during the downward swing of the economy.

The conscious application of such theories in Britain since 1946 certainly helped to gain a twenty-five year respite in which 'full employment' was declared government policy, and the fluctuations of the old days were replaced by government-influenced 'stops' and 'goes' in the economy according as its movements tended to speed up or slow down.

It is now clear that, although it lasted some twenty-five years, the respite for Britain was temporary. Despite *The Guardian*'s assertion that Marx has been 'proved wrong', current developments in Britain and the capitalist world as a whole make topical once again his theory of the 'general crisis' of capitalism.

In this connection, it is well to note that just prior to the world economic crisis of 1929–30, economists and politicians all over the world were chorusing that Marx was wrong. In those days the businessman Henry Ford was held up as the Messiah of the capitalist system. The world crisis came soon after. It is ironical that, almost contemporarily with the articles quoted above from *The Guardian* and *The Economist*, the present incumbent of the Ford throne visited Britain to inform us that he would not build a new automobile works here, but go elsewhere where profits were likely to be greater.

In the 1920s, the Ford 'miracle' was counterposed to Marxism. Then came the world economic crisis. Today, again, the orthodox school still relies on 'miracles', and we read the words of Samuelson as follows:

'The miracles of sustained growth in production and living standards have taken place in the second-level countries—Japan, Germany, Italy, France, Scandinavia, Western Europe generally ... The growth experience of the years 1950–70 revealed that a market economy enriched by government planning and micro-economic control could perform favourably in comparison to past epochs of both capitalist and communist development.' (Samuelson, op. cit., p. 712.) And again, some pages later, tribute is paid to the West German 'miracle'. (Ibid., p. 819.)

If Samuelson's miracular economics had included also a detailed survey of the 'miracles' of the USSR's post-war recovery, and of the developments in the German Democratic Republic, Hungary, Poland and all the other socialist countries—whatever their weaknesses—we could accept his approach as objective. But as it is, we can only label it as one-sidedly orthodox. Also, the 'miracles' he mentions are already proving to be not as stable as they were.

Marx wrote Vol. I of *Capital* in the years preceding 1867. In 1886 in his preface to the first English edition, Engels wrote:

'The time is rapidly approaching when a thorough examination of England's economic position will impose itself as an irresistible national necessity. The working of the industrial system of this country, impossible without a constant and rapid extension of production' (the modern 'growth rate') 'and therefore of markets, is coming to a dead stop. . . . Foreign industry, rapidly developing, stares English production in the face everywhere. . . . Surely, at such a moment, the voice ought to be heard of a man whose whole theory is the result of a life-long study of the economic history and condition of England, and whom that study led to the conclusion that, at least in Europe, England is the only country where the inevitable social revolution might be affected entirely by peaceful and legal means.' (*Capital*, Vol. I, pp. 31–32.)

Engels wrote these words in 1886. They may have appeared to many to have been rendered obsolete in the successive phases following the First and Second World Wars. And yet, in 1971, Britain still faced a permanent crisis in obtaining foreign markets, and now, once again, after an unprecedented interval, the problem is as described by Engels, as deciding 'what to do with the unemployed'.

To quote once again from *The Economist* of 27 November 1971: 'For the past 25 years one probably reasonable, but unpopular, school of economic thought has been saying that what Britain needs is a short but sharp bout of unemployment and shakeout of labour. This cruel, but potentially very hopeful, situation has now been created.' Thus, in *The Economist*'s view, throughout the only period in British economic history when relatively 'full employment' has existed, one school of thought has consistently maintained the desirability of unemployment. This is simply Marx's 'surplus labouring population' as 'a condition of existence of the capitalist mode of production' since it provides 'a mass of human material always ready for exploitation'. (*Capital*, Vol. I, p. 693.) It is no accident that 'full employment' increased the bargaining power of trade unions, and therefore it is equally no accident that a school of orthodox economists has continually advocated a return to unemployment.

The other side of the same medal, as portrayed by Keynes in his *General Theory of Employment, Interest and Money* (1936) was the view that 'if nations can learn to provide themselves with full employment by their domestic policy . . . there need be no economic forces calculated to set the interest of one country against that of its neighbours.' (Op. cit., p. 382.) With this strictly *capitalist*-orientated formulation we may compare Marx's words in the *Communist Manifesto*: 'In proportion as the exploitation of one individual by another is put an end to, the exploitation of one nation by another will also be put an end to. In proportion as the antagonism between classes within the nation vanishes, the hostility of one nation to another will come to an end.'

Keynes saw this aim as being achieved by a capitalism that abolished unemployment. Marx saw it as being achieved by abolishing capitalism as such, this being necessary in order to abolish unemployment. Keynes' 'economic miracle' has been manifest in Britain for twenty-five years, but has now ended. Another proof that basically Marx was right after all?

In discussing economic crises under capitalism, Marx did not make the mistake of trying to pin them down to one single cause. He rather saw them as arising because of the anarchistic way capitalism develops, so that unevenness and disequilibrium are inevitable. True, if any ultimate cause had got to be singled out, then he found 'the last cause of all real crises always remains the poverty and restricted consumption of the masses as compared to the tendency of capitalist production to develop the productive forces in such a way, that only the absolute power of consumption of the entire society would be their limit'. (*Capital*, Vol. III, p. 568.)

But this must not be taken as a crude under-consumption theory, for Marx stressed that 'it is not a fact that too many necessities of life are produced in proportion to the existing population. The reverse is true. Not enough is produced to satisfy the wants of the great majority decently and humanely. . .

'In the first place too large a portion of the population . . . are dependent through force of circumstances on the exploitation of the labour of others, or compelled to perform certain kinds of labour . . . under a miserable mode of production. In the second place, not enough means of production are produced to permit the employment of the entire able-bodied population under the most productive conditions. . .

'On the other hand, there is periodically a production of too many means of production and necessities of life to permit of their serving as means for the exploitation of the labourers at a certain rate of profit . . . that is, too many to permit of the continuation of this process without ever recurring explosions.' (Ibid., pp. 302–3.)

This tendency to 'overproduce', within the context of profitability, must be viewed as affecting both capital and population alike. Thus, 'the course characteristic of modern industry, viz., a decennial cycle (interrupted by smaller oscillations), or periods of average activity, production at high pressure, crisis and stagnation, depends on the constant formation, the greater or less absorption, and the re-formation of the industrial reserve army of surplus population' (Ibid., Vol. I, p. 694.), or, in contemporary language, the 'unemployed' and the 'redundant'.

Now the reason why, according to Marx, a periodic return to unemployment is inevitable, is that: 'The capitalist mode of production . . . comes to a standstill at a point determined by the production and realisation of profit, not by the satisfaction of social needs.' (Ibid., Vol. III, p. 303.) In addition, as we have already seen, there is a general tendency for the rate of profit to fall, even though firms can offset this tendency to some extent by monopolistic price policies.

The same basic idea is again expressed as follows: 'The greatest part of the producers (the workers) are non-consumers (non-buyers) of a very considerable part of their product,' they 'can only consume an equivalent for their product as long as they produce more than this equivalent-surplus value or surplus product. They must always be *over-producers*, must always produce over and above their needs, in order to be able to be consumers or buyers within the limits of their needs.' (*Theories of Surplus Value*, pp. 397–8.) So that a crisis will at the same time be 'a superfluity of all things needed for production' and on the other hand 'a superfluity of all kinds of unsold commodities on the market'. At the same time, 'bankrupt capitalists and hungry workers'. (Ibid., p. 401.)

Britain opens the 1970s with several major failures of large companies; a record figure for capital investment abroad; and a record figure since 1945 for unemployment. Marx's 'model' is confirmed by real life. And stocks and shares boomed as unemployment rose.

Another angle relevant to the recurring crises of capitalism, or simply, the 'general crisis', is what has come to be called the balance between spending and investment, or what Marx, long before, had identified as Departments 1 and 2 in production: '1. Means of Production . . . 2. Means of Consumption', (a division which has always played a major role in Soviet planning. By means of an exhaustive analysis (*Capital*, Vol. II, p. 457f.) Marx showed how, under capitalism, maladjustments were inevitable between these two Departments. And, he warned, if one were simply to say 'the working class receive too small a portion of their own product, and the evil would be remedied by giving them a larger share of it, or raising their wages, we should reply that crises are precisely always preceded by a period in which wages rise generally and the working class actually get a larger share of the annual product intended for consumption . . . It seems, then, that capitalist production comprises certain conditions which are independent of good or bad will and permit the working class to enjoy that relative prosperity only momentarily, and at that always as a harbinger of a coming crisis'. Besides the division into Departments I and II, there must be added a further division, 'between the production of necessities of life and that of luxuries,' a division which 'touches the character and the quantitative conditions of production to their very roots.' (Ibid., p. 476.)

Essentially, the point which Marx makes is that the forces at work under capitalism inevitably do not produce an equilibrium between Departments I and II, nor an equilibrium between supply and demand for consumers' goods, nor an equilibrium between supply and demand for luxuries.

Throughout his work, Marx takes production as the central activity and the source of surplus-value. He recognises also the importance of exchange and trade, but treats them as having a subordinate role. However, at times this role may become dominant because 'all nations with a capitalist mode of production are seized periodically by a feverish attempt to make money without the mediation of the process of production'. (Ibid., p. 64.) This involves dealings in credit and, says Marx, 'as soon as the development of credit interferes, the relation between originally advanced capital and capitalist surplus-value is still more complicated'. (Ibid., p. 368.)

In addition to maladjustments in production, there are periodical maladjustments in credit and trading policy. So long as the process of reproduction is in flow . . . credit lasts and extends . . . As soon as a stoppage takes place, in consequence of delayed returns, overstocked markets, fallen prices, there is a superfluity of industrial capital, but it is in a form, in which it cannot perform its functions. It is a mass of commodity-capital, but it is unsaleable . . . Credit is contracted, (1) because this capital is unemployed . . . (2) because confidence in the continuity of the process of reproduction has been shaken; (3) because the demand for this commercial credit decreases.' (Ibid., Vol. III, p. 567.)

Marx noted that foreign trade could act as a relief to manufacturers in disposing of goods unsaleable at home. But here, too, limitations could arise in the market and goods remain unsold. 'The manufacturer may actually sell to the exporter, and the exporter may in turn sell to his foreign customer, the importer may sell his raw materials to the manufacturer, and the manufacturer his products to the wholesale dealer, etc. . . . But at some particular and unseen point, the goods may lie unsold. On some occasions again, the supply of all producers and middlemen may become generally overstocked. . . A crisis occurs whenever the returns of these merchants, who sell at long range, or whose supplies have accumulated on the home market, become so slow and meagre, that the banks press for payment . . . It is then that forced sales take place . . . And then we have the crash.' (Ibid., pp. 359–60.)

One more passage from Marx on crises is worth noting, especially as it is more than 100 years old, and modern experience confirms his words:

'On the eve of a crisis, and during its sway, commodity capital' (the orthodox today would say 'capital goods') 'in its capacity as a potential money-capital is contracted. It represents less money-capital for its owner and his creditors (likewise as a security for bills of exchange and loans), than it did at the time when it was bought and when the discounts and loans made on it were transacted . . . Such a collapse of prices merely balances their inflation in preceding periods.

'The incomes of the unproductive classes, and of those, who live on fixed incomes, remain for the greater part stationary during the inflation of prices going hand in hand with an over-production and overspeculation. . .

'With reference to the imports and exports we remark, that all countries become successively implicated in a crisis, and that then it becomes evident, that all of them, with few exceptions, have imported and exported too much, so that there is a balance of payment against all of them. The trouble, therefore, is not with the balance of payment. For instance, England suffers from an export of gold. It has imported too much. But at the same time all other countries are overcrowded with English goods. They also have imported too much, or too much has been imported into them . . . The balance of payment is in times of general crisis against every nation, at least against every commercially developed nation, but always the one succeeding the other, like firing in squads, as soon as the turn of each comes for making payments . . . It then becomes evident, that all these nations have simul-taneously overexported (and overproduced) and overimported (and overtraded), that prices were inflated in all of them, and credit overdrawn. And the same collapse follows in all of them.' (Ibid., pp. 576–8.)

Much more could be quoted from Marx on crises, but enough has been said, it is hoped, to show that he was not only in advance of his time, but that much of what he said is still relevant, though in many respects events have moved far beyond the stage of development with which he was familiar.

Essentially he saw capitalism as aiming at making profit in

order to accumulate capital, in order to make more profit. He did not see the *main* aim of capitalists as being to consume, but to grow richer. Hence the 'profit motive' is never separated by him from the accumulation of further capital.

While Marx always gave priority to production and accumulation of capital, he did not ignore exchange. And in his study of money, while he completely rejected any monetary theory that regarded money as being more important than production, he recognised that there was definitely a connection between the 'state of prices, quantity of circulating commodities, and velocity of money-currency' which he described as 'all variable'. (Ibid., Vol. I, p. 137.) On the other hand, he rejected the proposition that it is 'prices that are determined by the quantity of the circulating medium, and that the latter depends on the quantity of the precious metals in a country'. (Ibid., p. 139.) Money itself has a value. he said, 'only in so far as paper-money represents gold, which like all other commodities has value, it is a symbol of value'. (Ibid., p. 144.)

Marx's insistence on the importance of gold as the 'money-commodity' has led to considerable discussion among Marxists in view of the recent tendencies on a world scale to devise some new basis for international currencies. The crisis of the gold dollar on the one hand, and the initiating of Special Drawing Rights by the IMF, have raised the question whether, in the world today, money can at last become separated from its commodity basis in gold. In an article in the Moscow journal *World Economy and International Relations* in August 1971, the question of the possibility of 'paper gold' was raised. The writer, A. Eidelnant, said that 'the trend towards gold being ousted from money circulation and then from capitalism's currency system is undeniable' as also is 'the loss by gold of some of its classical functions'. The writer did not, however, venture any solution but a rise in the price of gold so that it could be a basis for a larger circulation of currency. Two other writers, Atlas and Matyukhin, in the same publication, referred to 'gold being pried out by paper currency' and the prevalence of 'credit money' which 'reduces distribution costs through the substitution of paper symbols of value for gold money'. And these writers conclude, after a detailed discussion of the problem, that 'no matter how the "new capitalism" may restrict and modify the functioning of gold as the money commodity . . . a real and fully-fledged substitute has not been devised yet'. Therefore, they state, gold still 'functions as genuine, objectively valid, universal money from which neither national nor international credit can fully emancipate themselves'.

When Lenin was writing, the development of monopoly had gone a long way since Marx's death. In *Imperialism*, he referred to the way in which imperialism 'complicates and accentuates the contradictions of capitalism, it "entangles" monopoly with free competition, but *it cannot abolish* exchange, the market, competition, crises, etc. . . . Not pure monopolies, but monopolies in conjunction with exchange, markets, competition, crises—such is the essential feature of imperialism in general . . . This combination of antagonistic principles, viz., competition and monopoly, is the essence of imperialism'.

In Britain from 1946 onwards, partly as a result of the work of Keynes and Beveridge, within the structure of capitalism, there was a 'full employment' policy for some twenty-five years which has now come to an end. This meant keeping the 'reserve army of labour' down to not more than $2\frac{1}{2}$ per cent, a policy never envisaged by Marx, though he would undoubtedly have taken the view that, however long it lasted, it was but a palliative.

It is significant that Samuelson, in the book already quoted, heads one section with the words: 'The Crisis of Capitalism?' He then comments that 'a quarter of a century ago a failure of nerve was becoming evident in the West'. (Samuelson, op. cit., p. 818.) This is from the 8th edition, dated 1970. Can anyone honestly maintain that since 1970 there is not even more evidence of 'failure of nerve' in the West than twenty-five years earlier?

In *The Times Business News* of 30 December 1971, this was made very clear in an article by T. F. Cripps and Professor W. B. Reddaway who wrote: 'Productivity has improved much faster than in the previous decade' but 'employees have suffered large-scale redundancies.' While 'productivity has been rising at an unusually fast rate' on the other hand 'output has grown more slowly, on average, since 1965.'

Hence we are back once again with one of the basic contradictions of capitalism: growing production on the one hand, but growing unemployment on the other. Characteristically enough Cripps and Reddaway only see one solution: 'The implication is that productivity growth has been unusually rapid and that if an increase in unemployment were to have been avoided output would have had to rise faster, not slower, than in earlier years.'

In advocating this 'solution' the writers ignore a quite obvious alternative way out—not because they are bad economists—but because under capitalism it is simply not practicable. It is this: If every Productivity Agreement were so drafted that all increased *productivity* had to be carried forward into increased *production*, making nobody redundant and passing on the benefit of the increased productivity to the consumer, then, and then only, could increased productivity be fully utilised in the form of increased *production*. Only then would the maximum benefit be achieved for the level of production.

But under capitalism, especially monopoly capitalism, this would not be profitable business. Hence the dilemma of rising productivity and rising unemployment. Under socialist planned systems it is possible to ensure simultaneously rising productivity, rising production, full employment, and steadily rising earned incomes with or without falling prices.

The dilemma can only be solved by a socialist planned economy. This is one reason why capitalism can *not* 'beat Karl Marx'.*

---

* See also *Postscript*, p.171.

CHAPTER EIGHT

'Free Enterprise', 'Consumers' Sovereignty' and Planning

Although the first State Plan of a comprehensive character was introduced in the USSR in 1928, it took until after the Second World War for the teaching of Economics in Britain even to recognise that state economic planning had come to stay and was an essential fact of world economic life.

As Cairncross points out: 'Once a country regards the rate of growth as something over which it can exercise at least a limited degree of control, and seeks to reorient its policies with a view to faster growth it is well on the way to accepting the need for economic planning in some form.' (Cairncross, op. cit., p. 554.)

Before the Second World War it would be true to say that, in the main, the economists of the West either totally ignored, or even sneered at, the planned economy of the USSR. There were however a few socialistically-inclined exceptions such as Barbara Wootton, G. D. H. Cole and Maurice Dobb, by whom socialist and planning ideas were taken seriously. It was in that period that Maurice Dobb wrote his *Planning and Capitalism* in which he showed how the contrast between the world economic crisis and the USSR's Five Year Plan had made the word 'planning' almost 'a magic formula'. But this entailed 'a good deal of confused thinking . . . ranging from proposals to build bigger and stronger private monopolies in industry' (continued in the 'merger-mania' of subsequent Labour governments at the end of the 1960s) 'to more genuinely socialist schemes for the nationalisation of industry. In between stood a varied assortment of schemes

for benevolent state control of investment and the financing of
"public works"'. (Dobb, op. cit., p. 7.) And, while final judgement was deferred by Dobb to the future, he concluded that at
that time capitalist '"planning" . . . operates so as to strengthen
capitalist monopoly rather than to tame it, and that it represents
the calling in of the State to reinforce the attempts which the big
monopoly-groups have made to restrict competition and control
prices. In other words, it has been *planning for restriction*, not for
progress and plenty'. (Ibid., pp. 12–13.) These words, applied to
the 1970s, express precisely what Marxists regard as the true aim
behind the campaign to draw Britain into the European Common
Market.

Harvey (op. cit., pp. 12, 307, 309) describes 'collectivism' in
these words: 'Here the State assumes responsibility for estimating
people's wants. It owns the factors of production' and directs
their use. It 'decides what proportion of productive resources
shall be devoted to the accumulation and maintenance of capital,'
matters which, under capitalism, are left to 'individual entrepreneurs'. Again, the state 'decides how much to save and invest.
Saving is "forced" by some form of taxation.' Under 'capitalism,
however, decisions regarding saving and investment are left to
private individuals'—and a fine mess they make of it if left to
themselves, as we might paraphrase Keynes as showing!

Harvey was writing in 1968 in a reprint corrected and up-to-
date, and it is hardly excusable that in this connection he should
have ignored the fact that nowadays a British Chancellor of the
Exchequer invariably takes into account the saving and spending
of consumers. Moreover, if Harvey had studied a sample budget
from the USSR he would have seen that state revenue comes
overwhelmingly from the economy, not from taxation, and that it
provides the resources for investment. (See *supra.*, p. 73.) The
use of such terms as 'profit' and 'turnover tax' in this context are
purely a matter of nomenclature. The essential point is that the
difference between the total flow of consumers' goods on the one
hand (Department 2 of production) and the total flow of producers' goods on the other (Department 1) are deliberately planned

to meet what are considered to be the best interests of the community, present and future together. To pose 'forced saving' as a characteristic of socialism in distinction from capitalism, especially British capitalism during the years of inflation, is quite unsound.

Cairncross (op. cit., p. 557) puts the issue more clearly when he writes:

'In framing its plans the government may follow one or another of two courses. It may allow consumer spending to influence what is to be produced without itself planning production; or it may leave the consumer free to spend his money as he chooses, but only on such products as are allowed to reach the market. The first alternative is the one adopted under a system of private enterprise, which confers on a great many individual producers the power to decide how the factors of production shall be employed' subject to the 'compulsions' of the market. The second alternative 'involves comprehensive economic planning by the State and the setting up of production targets that may bear little or no relation to current market shortages or surpluses'. (This, of course, is true in cases of bad planning, or decisions made under pressures outside purely economic considerations. But it can also be true where good planning demands substantial provision for future development.)

On Britain, Cairncross says: 'In a country like ours . . . decisions that might otherwise rest with a central planning authority take shape instead in the market . . . lubricated by the expenditure of consumers.' (Ibid., p. 11.)

His summary of the difference between the two systems reaches fundamentals: 'The two main features of capitalism are the private ownership of property and freedom of enterprise . . . associated with . . . above all, class divisions. The ownership and control of property is heavily concentrated in the hands of a comparatively small class of persons'. (Ibid., p. 189.) But whereas this is almost an aside in Cairncross' outlining of the problem, it is the core of Marx's.

But for a classical textbook case of bias on the subject we may mention Benham. For here 'planning' is made totally

H

arbitrary: 'Under a system of complete central planning, one person or committee would act as economic dictator . . . who would be compelled to make the final decisions. Only a superman could avoid making many mistakes . . . Those who are bent on mob oratory and political intrigue are not necessarily those best qualified to plan and control the economic life of the country . . . Decisions to save and decisions to invest are the same decisions, made at the same time by the same person, the economic dictator'. In contrast, capitalism offers 'freedom or choice by consumers'. (*Benham's Economics*, pp. 44, 45, 70.)

It will be noted from the above that 'a person or committee' is miraculously transformed into a personal 'economic dictator', a 'superman' if that were possible, 'bent on mob oratory and political intrigue'. And yet, to judge by all the newspaper comments on Mr Brezhnev and his other colleagues in the leadership of the USSR today, they are precisely not the type of bogy that Benham conjures up, but rather, in British journalese, 'technocrats.' In fact, the sort of men who, because of their wide experience of practical work, are best equipped, working collectively, to hammer out the most appropriate economic plans.

Contrary to Mr Benham's dream, there are in the USSR today, and in the other socialist countries, an enormous number of planning authorities, from the State Planning Commissions at the top (not 'dictators' but large and highly qualified bodies of men) to the planning department in every economic enterprise. Parallel with this structure are the Ministries of Finance, with their departments at all levels throughout the economic system. It is nowhere a matter for individuals to make decisions unless, as happens also with us on a Royal Commission or Board of Directors, the chairman's word is so influential that he usually carries the day. During the later lifetime of Stalin, this position did rule in the USSR in a number of organisations, but that is now regarded as an unfortunate episode in Soviet history, and by no means as a model system of working.

It is an unfortunate characteristic of almost all orthodox economics writers that they tend to pose the 'individual' consumer or 'individual' firm as typical of capitalism and the 'State' as typical of socialism. But to write of ICI or Unilever or Barclays Bank as an 'individual' firm is quite as misleading as to refer to a 'trade union' as an individual worker. In both cases we are dealing with 'legal persons', but at that the individuality ends. Vast industrial 'firms' today are international in their ramifications, enjoying monopolistic or partially monopolistic powers and influence, varying according to the particular market. Sometimes they have, in one country, to contend against local competition, or competition from a firm from yet another country; while in other cases they enjoy more or less exclusive monopoly rights, sometimes by agreement, sometimes by hazard. Hence, to talk of 'free enterprise' as synonymous with freedom for 'individual' producers tends to exaggerate the role of the individual under capitalism.

This is also so when we regard the individual as a consumer. For, when the merits of the 'free market' system are outlined, we find that its limitations are invariably played down in the textbooks. These limitations may be reduced basically to three:

(1) The existence of monopoly, oligopoly and imperfect competition. All these possibilities, typical of the economic world today under capitalism, detract from the original theoretical purity of 'perfect competition'—the abstract model in which price is kept down to marginal costs of production (in orthodox terminology) or near to value (in Marxist terminology). And if such perfect competition does not apply, then that tendency for the 'free economy' to *keep prices down* disappears.

(2) The existence of advertising on its contemporary scale: Right up to the present day the Theory of Value is still taught within orthodox economics as if Supply, Demand and Price were three independent variables. On this assumption, price is said to be determined by supply and demand, reaching 'equilibrium' at the point where they are equal and opposite, i.e., at which all supplies are sold.

This theory, and its diagrammatical representation, still dominates the textbooks, though some have now added the discussion of indifference curves which are detailed examinations of the order of consumer preferences.

But whether the traditional supply and demand curves, or indifference curves, are favoured; in either case it is assumed that the consumer is an autonomous agent 'freely' expressing his wants.

This, however, is no longer true, if it ever was. For the advertising of products is now an important aspect of salesmanship, and the aim of advertising is to condition consumer demand to suit the needs of the supplier. Now that advertising can amount to as much as 25 per cent of the 'cost' of a product, it is quite impermissible to treat Supply and Demand curves as independent. The fact of modern advertising is that demand may be increased more by spending a given sum on advertising than on price cuts. This means that, instead of stimulating demand by lowering price, as still presented in the classical diagram, firms get the same effect, more cheaply, by spending less on advertising than the loss that would be suffered by reducing price. There is theremore no longer an independent consumers' demand curve for an advertised product. How many women realise, for example that 25 per cent of what they pay to cover the 'cost' of their cosmetics is, in fact, being paid by them to cover the cost of persuading them to demand that particular kind of cosmetic?

To be realistic in the modern world, Supply, Demand and Price should in many cases be diagrammatically represented only with the additional inclusion of advertising costs and their result on the slope and position of the Demand Curve. But up to now orthodox economics has tended to turn a blind eye, rather as, in the past, it evaded public enterprise and monopoly long after these had become permanently installed as a normal feature in economic life.

However, in so far as it is now proved that producers do in fact 'create demand' for their products by indoctrinating consumers; one more concession has been made to Marx who long ago maintained that it was the capitalist producer, in his striving for profit, who really had the initiative in our economic system.

It remains a fact, of course, that both under capitalism and socialism there is always an ultimate consumers' veto on any product that is so bad that—even with advertising—there is no effective demand for it. Such unsold useless products are casualties of the 'market' under capitalism, and casualties of 'defective planning' under socialism. At least, to this extent, the consumer's veto remains, for, as Marx pointed out in *Capital*, labour 'does not count . . . if a thing is useless.' (Marx, op. cit., Vol. I, p. 48.)

(3) Finally, the 'free price system' is based on people's ability to spend, and this is not equal. It depends on income, and this in turn greatly depends on whether the income is 'earned' or 'unearned', derived from labour or from property.

So long as there are large disparities of income, the well-off consumers will have greater effective choice than the badly-off. If in fact market prices affect production, then production will be biased in favour of meeting the wants of the wealthy. To suggest that 'market demand' is an effective way of expressing *majority* wants in such a situation has no foundation in fact. Therefore the view that wants could be more democratically assessed than by money demand is a tenable one, and undermines the traditional case for a 'market economy'.

When we take together the three defects of the market economy here outlined; monopoly, conditioning of consumers by advertising, and the unequal pull of consumers according to their income, we find that the 'free market' is not at all as 'free' as the term would suggest.

When, in contrast, orthodox economists turn to Planned Economies, they immediately start to calculate 'costs' which, when dealing with 'free economies' they tend simply to leave out of account. To make a symmetrical comparison, the cases of faulty planning—which undoubtedly exist—must be measured against the costs of unplanned economies including such 'adjustments' as bankruptcies, waste and unsold products, idle capital, unemployment and so on. Only if all these actual *costs* of capitalism are taken into account does it even begin to be possible to draw up any sort of scientific balance sheet between the two systems. Unfortunately, this is hardly ever attempted in the field of orthodox economics.

It has often been commented that Marx never studied in detail what would happen once capitalist society had been superseded by public ownership, collectivism or communism. This is true, because his detailed work was to analyse the capitalism within which he lived. He saw this as engendering habits of co-operation among the working class, both at work and in trade unions, which would give them the sort of co-operative experience necessary for the running of an economic system collectively. As to the rest, Marx asserted certain principles, but left the details for experience to decide. In Chapter 5 we saw how, at the time at which he wrote, Marx dealt with the question of the distribution of the social product under the new economic system. We referred there mainly to his analysis in the *Critique of the Gotha Programme.*

Again, in Vol. III of *Capital* he returned briefly to the theme with the words that 'after the abolition of the capitalist mode of production, but with social production still in vogue, the determination of value continues to prevail in such a way that the regulation of the labour-time among the various groups of production, also the keeping of accounts in connection with this becomes more essential than ever'. (Op. cit., p. 992.) And again: 'Only when production will be under the conscious and pre-arranged control of society will society establish a direct relation between the quantity of social labour employed in the production of definite articles and the demand of society for them.' (Ibid., p. 221.)

But when it comes to the subject of *planning*, nowadays inextricably bound up with discussions of Socialism and Communism, Marx was relatively silent. This was not because he opposed planning, for he clearly favoured a planned economic system as against the anarchical system of capitalism, but mainly because the detailed structure of the 'communist' society of the future was for the people of the future to work out for themselves. Nevertheless, this aspect of the subject was pursued slightly further by Engels.

Marx's lifetime collaborator, Frederick Engels, published his *Anti-Duhring* some six years before Marx's death, at a time when both their minds were working in very close harmony. In this book Engels elaborated the joint view of Marx and himself on socialist planning in the future, visualising 'a society which makes possible the harmonious co-operation of its productive forces on the basis of one single vast plan' which will 'allow industry to settle in whatever form of distribution over the whole country is best adapted to its own development and the maintenance of development of the other elements of production'. (Op. cit., p. 331.)

Under such a 'social plan . . . no individual can put on to others his share in productive labour' and 'productive labour, instead of being a means to the subjection of men, will become a means in their emancipation, by giving each individual the opportunity to develop and exercise all his faculties, physical and mental, in all directions: in which, therefore, productive labour will become a pleasure instead of a burden'. (Ibid., p. 331.)

At such a stage of development 'the appropriation by society of the means of production will put an end not only to the artificial restraints on production which exist today, but also to the positive waste and destruction of productive forces and products which is now the inevitable accompaniment of production and reaches its zenith in crises.' (Ibid., p. 317.) But even in advanced socialist (communist) societies 'it will be necessary for society to know how much labour each article of consumption requires for its production. It will have to arrange its plan of production in accordance with its means of production, which include, in particular, its labour forces. The useful effects of the various articles of consumption, compared with each other and with the quality of labour required for their production, will in the last analysis determine the plan'. (Ibid., p. 246.)*

---

* From the above passages (and there are others) it is quite clear that Marx and Engels considered that in the communist society of the future value would still be relevant at least as regards how much labour goes into the production of this or that product. Joan Robinson, having pointed to the uselessness of the Labour Theory of Value as a *price* theory under modern capitalism, suggests that it might 'come into its own under

But it was in the *Critique of the Gotha Programme* that Marx went furthest in his outline of how the products of society would be distributed under 'communism', the first stage of which is nowadays known by Marxists as 'socialism', entailing the public ownership and planning of the use of the means of production, but not yet that age of plenty in which each can receive according to need. Here Marx analyses what happens to 'total social product' in the new society, as we have already outlined in Chapter 5.

'What we have to deal with here is a communist society . . . as it *emerges* from capitalist society', and at this stage 'the individual producer receives back from society—after the deductions have been made—exactly what he gave to it.' Only later, in the age of plenty arising from a great increase in the productive forces, will distribution according to needs come about.

When Marx's prognostications are compared with the Soviet Constitution, there is a striking similarity. If there are differences in detail, these can be mainly traced to the fact—unforeseen by Marx—that the new social system has had for more than half a century to exist in a hostile world, and therefore has had to safeguard its *defence*. Apart from this, the economic foundation is described as 'the socialist system of economy and the socialist ownership of the instruments and means of production, firmly established as a result of the liquidation of the capitalist system of economy, the abolition of private ownership of the instruments of production, and the elimination of the exploitation of man by man'. (*USSR Constitution*, Art. 4.) It should be noted that the word 'exploitation' is used here in the economic sense of employment for private profit. As to the more sophisticated use of 'exploitation', in the psychological sense, this does not enter into the Marxist vocabulary though a case could certainly be made out for more investigation into the problem of power once a socialist state is established.

socialism'. Paul Mattick, commenting, dogmatically asserts that 'Marx had no such belief'. But the above sentences support Robinson as against Mattick. (See Mattick, *Marx and Keynes*, p. 313.)

Taking the USSR as the prototype of the countries with Marxist Governments it is worth noting several other features:

Economic life 'is determined and directed by the state national-economic plan, with the aim of increasing the public wealth, of steadily raising the material and cultural standards of the working people, of consolidating the independence of the USSR and strengthening its defensive capacity'. (Ibid., Art. II.) Indeed, it was primarily due to this latter reason that the First Five Year Plan was responsible for 'the setting up of production targets that (bore) little or no relation to current market shortages', as Cairncross said. (See *supra*, p. 105.) The fact remains that for all countries defence is a drain on the economy, though it can be a very profitable 'drain' under capitalism, and the less advanced a country is, the more this is complicated by the need for allocations for growth and development. The greater the 'deductions' (to use Marx's word) for such purposes, the less there can be available at any one time for consumers' goods or social services.

The early Five Year Plans of the USSR, and of other socialist countries, have all testified to the fact that the importance of the 'portion for the expansion of production' (Marx's phrase) or 'the aim of increasing public wealth' (Soviet phrase) have always meant some restriction on the rate at which living standards could be raised at any particular time.

Nevertheless, in a planned economy it is possible to guarantee work for all, equal pay for men and women and old and young for similar work; and a limited working day and paid minimum holidays for all.

The Soviet trade unions by law enjoy many rights within the productive system, including the right to veto the dismissal of any one of their colleagues. Moreover, regular production conferences now take place in every enterprise so that mass participation in the drawing up and carrying out of all plans is made possible. As a result, the Plans are no mere dictate from above, but are adopted by the appropriate committees at every level, while at the lowest level, at the point of production itself, regular Production Conferences play a decisive role.

The extent to which methods are effective, of course, can vary greatly from enterprise to enterprise, and the personal characteristics of both managers and trade union officials can be reflected in the quality and level of participation which takes place. But this is equally true of any democratic procedure in any country whatsoever, and in this respect there is no difference as regards the socialist countries.

In all the countries whose governments base themselves on Marxist Political Economy, planned production for the present and future welfare of the community is general. This takes the place of private profit as the motive for production. This means that a constant balance has to be achieved between satisfying present and future needs; and current production of goods and services has to be increased at the same time as resources are being set aside for future production. It is inevitable therefore, that as far as resources are allocated for future production, they cannot satisfy present consumers' wants. But as far as current goods and services are concerned, the socialist countries are more concerned that these should provide the maximum satisfaction of the community than any conglomeration of private suppliers (intent on their profits) in a market economy. Indeed, consumers' choice unadulterated by tendentious advertising is likely to be a more genuine choice than if it is influenced by the suppliers. Advertising in the socialist countries exists, but of a strictly informative character.

Whatever the criticisms of the planned economies, there is nowadays little doubt even among their critics that as regards working conditions, social services, care of children, education, health, and the rate at which housing is being developed, they have entered upon a new course of development.

True, a minimum of 'welfare' began to be introduced in Britain in the Liberal reforms of 1911. But it should be noted that our own *contributory* National Health followed our alliance with the USSR between 1941 and 1946, whereas a *free* Health Service had been a feature of the USSR since 1918. Although we preceded the Russians in achieving a universal system of elementary education, there seems to be little doubt that since 1946 one of the motives for our large-scale spending on technical colleges and new universities was, apart from purely domestic factors, the 'cold war' view that we must 'keep up with the Russians'.

The fact that socialism was first introduced in a backward country has certainly raised many problems. Internally, many economic tasks had to be performed which, in Marx's original anticipation, were to have been accomplished by capitalism. This fact, and the great burden of defence with which the USSR has had to saddle itself since 1917, have slowed down the rate of progress compared with what it might otherwise have been under a planned economy. But the basic dichotomy remains, between capitalism's production for private profit as its dominant feature, and socialism's planned production for community consumption and advance, which is the basic feature of the alternative system. In the one, the striving for surplus-value remains the driving force, while in the other it is a balanced growth affecting both means of consumption and means of production simultaneously.

It would be foolish to try to maintain that, under planning, errors of judgement or miscalculations are impossible. Of course they are possible, but the aim is so to improve planning techniques that the defects may, in due course, be eliminated. Under private enterprise errors of judgement and miscalculations are also possible. Moreover they are accepted as an intrinsic part of the system, to be 'ironed out' in due course by the 'higgling of the market'. In the one case there is an attempt, by planning more efficiently, to eliminate economic error, wrong forecasts or misuses of resources. In the other such defects are the raw material which the market economy has to deal with.

The *antithesis* between 'individual enterprise' and 'state planning', when we go into it, is to a considerable extent illusory. The individual under capitalism is less free than the orthodox economic myth would have us think; and under a planned economy the individual is a great deal more free than the same sources suggest.

Even if we consider the 'freest' of all in the capitalist system, the 'top people' who control its most gigantic enterprises, we find that they have to operate within limits imposed by the set-up of their companies, markets, raw materials, capital and labour. The law, too, to the individual tycoon may act as a substantial drag on freedom.

The difference in the case of socialist enterprise is not so great. Here too the 'top people' are limited by the objective conditions in which they are working. They have, it is true, the possibility of rising to the highest position in the State in their particular branch of the economy, strictly on the basis of ability; but on the other hand they are more subject to criticism from below than is the case anywhere within the rules of capitalist enterprise. Movement up and down the ladder of careers is much more flexible in the planned economies than under capitalism, since at no point whatsoever is any managerial or administrative official 'anchored' to his claim to a job through having 'money in the firm'. This is not to say that all capitalist chairmen and directors are not capable; but it does mean that in many cases the opportunity for their ability to flourish has been linked with capital investment which has led to, or been combined with, a share of administrative control.

As for consumers' freedom, the limits to consumers' choice are first, income, and second, the assortment available to choose from.

But whilst in the planned economies incomes are paid according to work, the capitalist economy has its two categories of incomes, from work and from property. The really large incomes come from the latter category.

When we come to assortment, it is undoubtedly true that, in any country which is deliberately planning capital accumulation for the future, there will be some limit on current consumption. The more backward a country is, the more effort has to be made to overcome this backwardness, and this means a high proportion of the national income being devoted to future production.

Nevertheless, there may still remain a large choice before individuals without coming anywhere near the scope of 'choice' allegedly provided by capitalism. How much, for example, do the contents of packets in Britain differ nowadays, despite the variety of names, labels, brands and prices? Is 'consumers' choice' really any better satisfied by having a variety of twenty different tooth pastes rather than, say five, all recommended by a Ministry of Health as positively beneficial? How many objects are bought in our shops nowadays, not because of their intrinsic use, but because sometime and somewhere the purchaser has read that he 'must have' this latest model?

A few years ago, when the USSR took part in London's Food Exhibition, it exhibited seventy varieties of bread which caused something of a sensation in the press, to which it had never occurred that a planned economy would turn out more than one or two types of loaf. In the USSR today, as resources become more abundant, increasing attention is being paid to consumers' choice, but within reason, not just to devise gimmicks that make a profit.

One of the generally agreed advantages of large-scale production, both to Marxists and to the orthodox, is that economies arise from scale, and that large-scale production means of necessity standardisation.

Whether consumers would have chosen this or not if the choice had ever been submitted to them, the fact is that in all developed countries today mass production of standardised products is a fact. Under capitalism, exceptions to this are still to be found in the more personal trades such as tailoring; yet an equally personal trade at one time, boot and shoe making, has now been almost completely taken over by large-scale firms.

The comparative lack of facilities for catering for personal needs has been more than once noted in the USSR, but it is significant that in all spheres dealing with arts and crafts there is a tendency to encourage co-operative production, so that traditional crafts may be kept alive but at the same time in such a way that the workers come together in co-operative work.

Another problem which has risen sharply in the socialist countries, and is intimately bound up with planning, is the limit to be set at any time to centralisation or, alternatively, decentralisation.

During the First Five Year Plan, and for many years after the Second World War, enterprises were being handed down from above more and more directives as to what they should produce. But not only what they should produce, but detailed specifications, quantities of raw materials, total labour employed, and so on were all incorporated in the central plans. Today it has been realised that this system of planning, which had grown like a mushroom from 1928 onwards, had completely outlived itself, and an 'Economic Reform' was introduced in 1965 which handed back to enterprises the power to decide for themselves all but about half a dozen main directives which had to be dovetailed into the national plan as a whole. In this way centralised planning goes on, but local adaptations to the needs of consumers are now much more possible than before.

It is relevant to quote here some of the arguments adduced by a socialist economist for socialist planning as against private enterprise. In *The Economic Theory of Socialism* (by O. Lange and F. M. Taylor), Lange sums up the Marxist case for planning in terms which, it would seem, are intelligible if not acceptable to the orthodox. Lange points out that socialism 'assumes freedom of choice in consumption', but that 'decisions of managers of production are no longer guided by the aim of maximising profit'. (Op. cit., p. 75.) The aim then becomes to minimise average cost while at the same time not letting prices run above marginal cost. (Ibid., p. 78.)

On the criticisms of Hayek, Robbins and others, that planning authorities would have a superhuman task in solving thousands, even millions of 'equations', Lange makes the point that basically the same equations have to be solved under capitalism. The criticisms he is here replying to are again reproduced in the textbooks by Harvey and Benham as we have already seen. In both socialism and capitalism, says Lange, the equations are solved by 'trial and error'. Under capitalism this is done 'in the market', but under a planning authority it should be more effectively done because 'the Central Planning Board has a much wider knowledge of what is going on in the economic system than any private entrepreneur can ever have'. (Ibid., p. 89.) Against the charge that there is no way, under planning, of giving proper 'accounting prices of capital goods and of productive resources in public ownership' he cites the American orthodox economist, Taussig, who dismissed such an argument as being of little weight as long ago as 1911. (Ibid., p. 90.)

Lange also makes a vital point concerning the social costs and benefits of production: A planned economy 'would evaluate *all* the services rendered by production and take into the cost accounts *all* the alternatives sacrificed . . . By doing so it would avoid much of the social waste connected with private enterprise . . . with much greater thoroughness.' (Ibid., p. 104.) It no longer is merely a matter of whether or not *a particular firm* hopes to gain a profit; but whether or not society as a whole stands to gain or lose from any suggested operation.

Today this is particularly relevant in relation to pollution, since at long last some degree of awareness has penetrated human consciousness on this matter. It is interesting to note that already when writing *Capital* Marx was aware of the problem and said:

'Capitalist production, by collecting the population in great centres, and causing ever-increasing preponderance of town population, on the one hand concentrates the historical motive-power of society; on the other hand, it disturbs the circulation of matter between man and the soil, *i.e.*, prevents the return to the soil of its elements consumed by man in the form of food and clothing; it therefore violates the conditions necessary to lasting fertility of the soil. By this action it destroys at the same time the health of the town labourer and the intellectual life of the rural labourer.' (Op. cit., Vol. I, p. 554.)

In the USSR during the first years of planning there is no doubt that the world's first socialist government, with an enormous expanse of undeveloped territory at its disposal, also collected the population in great centres and paid little attention to conservation. However, the situation has now changed, and energetic measures are now being undertaken to save Lake Baikal, one of the most interesting of the world's inland lakes, from the fate of the Great Lakes of Canada. The basic problem of Baikal is the economic one of developing the area as a source of timber, cellulose and wood pulp, while at the same time preserving the natural beauty of the area, the purity of its water, and its characteristic fauna and flora. These aims are now enshrined in legislation for the preserving of Baikal which are in line with general legislation on preserving the water resources of the USSR against pollution.

As to Marx's other point, the intellectual backwardness of the village, it has always been a matter of policy in the socialist countries to reduce by degree the 'contradiction between town and countryside', by raising rural living standards, material and cultural, at a rate more rapidly than in the towns until approximate equality is reached.

To return to Lange: on the question of whether public officials will be as efficient as privately-employed officials, Lange simply replies that if we compare state public officials under socialism with all the officials employed by all the large-scale businesses under capitalism there is not much difference. It does not, in fact, depend on the *ownership* but on the method by which they are paid. Economic officials in the socialist countries are paid, as far as this can be assessed, 'according to their work'. There is no reason at all why such a system, if effectively applied, should not produce the maximum efficiency.

Lastly, Lange raises the question whether the capitalist system is now compatible with economic progress. And he finds that, on balance, it is not, because 'the value of invested capital is not compatible with cost-reducing innovations'. And he quotes Professor Robbins (now Lord Robbins) to confirm the view that 'economic progress, in the sense of cheapening of commodities, is not compatible with the preservation of the value already invested in particular industries'. (Ibid., pp. 113–14.) Hence a tendency to hold back technical advance (a characteristic of monopoly recognised long ago), which in turn withholds capital from new fields in which it would be socially most productive though not 'profitable'. The marginal net productivity of capital is thus forced down, the point made by Keynes (see *supra.,* p. 54) and 'chronic unemployment of the factors of production results.' (Ibid., p. 115.) It is therefore natural that Lange opts for a rate of capital accumulation 'determined "corporately" in a socialist society' as likely to prove 'from the economic point of view, much more rational than the actual rate of saving in capitalist society.' (Ibid., p. 109.)

It should be admitted here that in the USSR, too, there has been resistance from managers of enterprises, struggling to fulfil planned targets, against replacing equipment by newer techniques until it is completely worn out. Moreover, time has been resented for installing new machinery. But to overcome this obstacle, the Economic Reform since 1965 has given greater incentives to improve efficiency, and greater autonomy to managers to make improvements. Since 'profit' in the Soviet economic system can only legally be obtained by reductions in cost due to greater productivity, the stress on profitability acts as a stimulus to raise efficiency within the framework of the Plan. The leading Soviet economist Alexander Birman has pointed out that the Soviet state has drastically reduced (from 40–50 to 5–6) 'the number of indices handed down to every enterprise as directives. Efforts have been made to improve prices, bank rates, incentive funds and the system of material responsibility. . . . Large-scale whole-sale trade in means of production' is being developed because 'it allows industrial enterprises to adapt quickly'. And 'centralised development and material incentive funds, formed from profit deductions, offer additional opportunities for every enterprise to promote plant modernisation and expend their activities for carrying out centralised plan assignments at minimum cost and maximum social benefit'. (Birman, 'Soviet Economic Reform', *New World Review*, New York, Winter 1971.)

The 'Economic Reform' in the USSR has had much publicity in the West, to the effect that it denotes a return to a 'market economy'. It is interesting to note that, on this point, Professor

I

Galbraith stands closer to the position of Birman, remarking that 'decentralisation' in the Soviet-type economies involves not a return to the market but a shift of some planning functions from the state to the firm'. (Galbraith, op. cit., p. 108.)

The free enterprise market economy is regarded, traditionally, as 'flexible'. The advantages of the adaptation of supply to demand are stressed by all orthodox economists, but it is much rarer to find one, like Professor Pigou, who shows the socially negative side of the balance sheet. Every 'adjustment' under capitalism, however costly, is invariably accepted as 'part of the system'. But when Planning gives rise to errors, or excessive costs, these are at once debited against the system as such with no attempt being made to equate them with analogous phenomena under capitalism.

As far as consumer's choice is concerned, the tendency is for the freedom of the consumer to be grossly overestimated under capitalism, and, on the other hand, to be grossly underestimated under Socialism.

It is hoped that the points made in this chapter will at least give rise to a more balanced view, with the recognition that, whatever problems it may have had to face and may still have to face, an economic system based on Marxism—that is, on public ownership and planning—has survival value in the modern world, and, in the long run at least, this need mean no disadvantage whatsoever, but rather advantage, to the average consumer.

CHAPTER NINE

Growth and Development

Before the Second World War the subject of economic growth and development received little attention from orthodox economists. To them, the main problems of real life tended to be unemployment, and the 'fluctuations' or 'cycles' of the economy which gave rise to it. The subject of the growth rate of the National Income was still more or less *terra incognita*. In contrast, Marx had always considered capitalism in its development, with the *accumulation* and *reproduction* of capital as its most essential feature. In modern orthodox terms, he was concerned with economic growth, even under the conditions of capitalism.

If we turn to Vol. II of *Capital* we find that Marx investigated in the greatest detail the process by which capital was accumulated and reproduced in a capitalist economy. He made a basic distinction, which plays a vital part in socialist planning today, between Department I and Department II of production, divided into means of production (capital goods) and consumers' goods.

In analysing the incomes arising from production in the two departments, Marx showed how wages were paid in both departments, while in each department the total wages earned fell below the amount of value produced by the amount of surplus-value accruing in rent, interest, profit and undistributed profits.

As far as wages as a whole are concerned, Marx assumed, and this assumption remains generally correct today despite small savings in the Post Office and elsewhere, that they were more or less entirely spent on the products of Department II. But as for the surplus value, while part of this was spent on consumption (both of necessities and luxuries) an important part was always returned to production in the form of additional capital. As Marx himself put it, 'these conditions become so many causes of abnormal movements, implying the possibility of crises, since a balance is an accident under the crude conditions of this production'. (Op. cit., p. 578.)

Approaching the same problem from a different angle, aiming at preserving capitalism rather than laying bare its innate faults, Keynes was in fact confronting the same basic phenomena when, within the context of credit only, he pointed to the unlikely coincidence of the rate of saving and the rate of investment (meaning spending on capital goods) under what Marx terms 'these crude conditions of production'. Keynes's disequilibrium which was likely to arise spontaneously between rates of saving and investment, and which were automatically corrected by the adjustment of the price level, was in fact a re-statement of Marx's earlier position, in which disequilibrium was bound to arise because in the main spending came from the wage-earners whereas investment came out of surplus-value. To Marx the *main* destiny of earned income was to be spent on consumption, while the *main* source of capital was surplus value (unearned income). Thus Marx, from the beginning, drew a sharp class distinction between the wage-earners on the one hand and the unearned-income receivers, property-owners or investors on the other. While Keynes treated 'savings' and 'investment' in a non-class context, and solely from the point of view of money and credit, Marx differentiated between the bulk of earned income as being spent on consumption, and the bulk of capital being provided out of surplus-value, i.e. unearned income.

Marx's analysis of the permanent state of disequilibrium of the system therefore centred on the different class roles of those who live by selling their labour on the one hand, and those who both live on, and invest part of, their surplus value on the other. Keynes's 'revolution' in orthodox economics may be said to have centred on saving, credit and investment, and to have gone as far as possible, without challenging the system as such, to work out methods of perpetuating its existence through limited state intervention. The whole idea of the State taking up the slack spontaneously generated by the capitalist economy, and offsetting it when necessary, has in fact had a considerable effect on many government policies since the Second World War. Admitting that capitalism, if left to itself, will not in fact adjust saving and investment so as to preserve equilibrium, Keynes advocated that the State should consciously act as a supplementary investor, or regulator of investment, so as to compensate for the vagaries of private capitalism as actuated by the profit motive. There is no doubt that his views, put forward in the 1920s, did give a shot in the arm to British capitalism after the Second World War and that Britain's policy of 'full employment' would never have been possible without a 'stop-go' credit policy based on Keynes's teaching.

However, at the beginning of the 1970s the Keynesian honeymoon (miracle?) is at an end, and the more basic contradictions, as exposed by Marx, are with us again.

Paul Baran pays the following tribute to Keynes, which includes the necessary limitations: 'Operating with the customary tools of conventional theory, remaining well within the confines of "pure economics", faithfully refraining from considering the socio-economic process as a whole, the Keynsian analysis advanced to the limits of bourgeois economic theorising, and exploded its entire structure. Indeed, it amounted to an "official" admission on the part of the "Holy See" of conventional economics that instability, a strong tendency towards stagnation, chronic under-utilisation of human and material resources, are inherent in the capitalist system.' (Baran, op. cit., pp. 7–8.)

Baran also quoted Joan Robinson, from an article in the *Economic Journal*, who put the matter in a nutshell: 'In the present age, any government which has both the power and the will to remedy the major defects of the capitalist system would have the will and the power to abolish it altogether, while governments which have the power to retain the system lack the will to remedy its defects'. (Ibid., p. 133.)

Hence, we may add, the stress of Marx, even *quâ* economist, on the importance of 'workers' power'.

Since 1946 two factors have obliged economists in the West to take into consideration the subjects of growth and development. First, there was the demonstration of the resilience of the Soviet planned economy under the impact of war. Secondly, there was the emergence after 1946 of a steadily lengthening list of newly independent countries, all of them 'underdeveloped', and all of them intent on developing their own economies with some degree of economic planning.

These changes in the world have begun to penetrate the economics textbooks. Samuelson, for example, writes that 'in the mid-twentieth century, preoccupation with development of poor regions and the challenge of Soviet growth rates have led to great concern over the questions: Is our own growth rate satisfactory? How can it be improved?' (Samuelson, op. cit., p. 797.)

Another economist, whose interest in the underdeveloped world has taken him well away from orthodoxy, Gunnar Myrdal, wrote in *Economic Theory and Under-Developed Regions*: 'Underdeveloped countries, utilising their newly won independent status, can by purposive policy interferences manage to alter considerably the direction of the market processes.

'There is a simple rule to apply . . . an underdeveloped country is well advised to take every and all measures which, on the ground of good reasoning, can be proved to enhance economic welfare, but it should carefully avoid policy measures which are not nationally beneficial in their total and ultimate effect.' There is thus introduced the concept of a 'national economic development plan . . . an overall, integrated national plan . . . all this amounts to something new in history' which 'cannot rationally be made in terms of the costs and profits of individual enterprises' because these 'cannot be expected to produce the product for sale at a competitive price'. Hence Myrdal sees the only road forward to lie in 'a compulsory rise in the share of the national income which is withheld from consumption and devoted to investment' (Myrdal, op. cit., pp. 66–87.) But he refrains from making a suggestion which Marxists would make, that such a policy should be operated in a way to weigh on the recipients of unearned rather than of earned incomes.

Another writer, Rene Dumont, also a specialist on development in underdeveloped countries, stresses the difficulties which arise from the various conceptions of 'planning'. He writes: 'Once rapid growth is made a fundamental objective, the most urgent means to implement it are still to be chosen. All Plans are first of all classifications of priorities'. And he points to two dangers: First, that plans may be elaborated over the heads of those who will have to carry them out, whereas success depends on 'the total involvement of government and people, the conscious choice of achievable goals and deliberate sacrifices.' The second danger, he says, is that the word 'plan' may be merely embodied in 'beautiful documents', or just be drafted to attract foreign aid. (R. Dumont, *False Start in Africa*, pp. 99–100.)

H. Myint, in *The Economics of the Developing Countries*, makes the point that it is not the 'initial drawing up of the economic development plans (frequently done with the assistance of foreign experts)' which is likely to present the greatest difficulty but 'the execution of the various projects according to a planned time-table and in keeping the different departments and agencies *continually informed*'. (Myint, op. cit., 3rd edn, p. 120.)

So the emergent countries, while attracted to growth and development, which in turn demands 'planning', have a number of possible problems: the devising of plans over the heads of those who must carry them out; the tendency for plans to be on paper only; and even if a plan is well conceived, there are the subsequent problems of co-ordination and communication.

They also have the problem of a shortage of economists of their own. And when the question of planning and growth arises, it is very doubtful if the capitalist countries—with their orthodox economics based on non-planned capitalism—are really in a position to render help. For, as Maurice Dobb has pointed out in his *Essay on Economic Growth and Planning*, 'the theories of economic growth recently in vogue among economists have been concerned almost exclusively with growth in capitalist economies where capital is in private ownership and investment predominantly under the control of private individuals and firms'. (Dobb, op. cit., p. 1.) It follows that when 'advisers' are poured into the underdeveloped countries, their approach to problems of economic growth and development is bound to be inextricably linked with the degree of orthodoxy of their capitalist or socialist economic background.

If any government in an underdeveloped country seriously adopts a policy of planning for economic growth and development, it is far more likely to be able to obtain sound advice from economists trained in countries where planned growth and development are actually taking place, than from orthodox economists from capitalist countries where planned growth is still rarely more than, as in some underdeveloped countries, 'beautiful documents'. It therefore comes about that a link is inevitably forged between governments of developing countries which are seriously concerned with planning, and the governments of those countries where planned growth and development are actually taking place; though taking place on the basis of the public ownership of the means of production.

A recent book from the USSR is of interest here, since it contains the views of writers who have grown up within the framework of a planned economy. Marx's contributions on the subject were meagre; much Soviet work has had to be of a pioneering character; but just because of this the Soviet Union may well be in a favoured position to assist others who are trying to plan their economic growth and development.

Four writers, Zhukhov, Delyushin, Iskanderov and Stepanov, published a joint work, *The Third World*, in 1970. In this book Stepanov writes that in the 'Third World, planning was borne into its economic life on the crest of the victorious independence movement'. He describes planning as 'the principle of conscious direction of economic processes' and thus 'the exact opposite of the traditional capitalist principle of free enterprise'. In the newly independent countries he sees development as necessitating some measure of planning, although in a number of countries this is still often 'toned down'. As a general rule 'feudal circles and big capitalists' lead the opposition to any form of state interference, but are not such a strong force in countries where the native capitalists themselves need state assistance to cope with their problems.

For the slowness with which development is actually taking place, this writer gives three reasons. First, the fact that 'the economic activities of millions, or rather tens and hundreds of millions, of small producers are not amenable to state regulation.' Then, the decisions of planning bodies tend to rely on 'prices, taxes, interest rates and other similar levers' which are 'in no way compulsory for the private sector,' and finally 'it is still hard to say just how far the governments of such countries consider themselves bound to adhere to the plans they themselves have adopted'.

A comparison of these views with those already quoted from Dumont and Myint shows that—at least in regard to the developing countries—there is considerable common ground between the 'Western' and 'Eastern' economists quoted. It is only fair to point out, however, that Dumont, Myint and Myrdal have all to a considerable extent, broken away from their orthodox tradition. Indeed, Myrdal actually advises citizens of underdeveloped countries to be wary of an economics that emanates from the capitalist countries because 'much of this theory is a rationalisation of the dominant interests in the industrial countries' and has not 'in the main . . . concerned itself with the problems of under-developed countries. If nevertheless it is uncritically applied to these problems, the theory becomes wrong'. (Myrdal, op. cit., p. 99.)

But if orthodox theory can 'become wrong' because of its genesis in the capitalist and imperialist system, to whom are the new countries to turn?—Clearly a system of Political Economy which has never been dedicated to upholding the capitalist system, but rather to making more understandable the causes of its instability, might be more likely to help.

The socialist countries, on the basis of a Marxism-Leninism which has always given due emphasis to the economic exploitation of colonialism and the fight against it, have had actual experience in planning their own economic growth and development. But their experience has been based on public ownership, whereas, in most of the underdeveloped countries, the question of property ownership is still unsettled. Cuba is an exception, where public ownership has now developed to the extent that Cuba is now accepted as one of the socialist countries. The United Arab Republic is a close runner-up, as since the nationalisation of the Suez Canal there has been a fairly continuous process of nationalisation, the introduction of planning, and close association with the countries under Marxist leadership. From these two at one end of the scale there is an endless gradation to countries which, even after independence, are still intent on preserving capitalist or pre-capitalist ownership. For example, in Ghana after the *coup* of 1966, deliberate steps were taken to reverse policies directed towards socialism, and, in keeping with this, vast areas of the country have now been farmed out to foreign capital. It is still too early to estimate whether the *coup* of 1972 will reverse this process. In general, the more a government leans towards socialism in its sympathies, so, internally, do we find attempts at public ownership and planning, and abroad an improvement of relations with the socialist states. On the other hand, where a capitalist course is adopted internally, so, too, relations are strengthened with foreign capital which inevitably means more foreign private investment attracted into the country.

The late Kwame Nkrumah, while still President of Ghana, wrote that 'although aid from socialist countries still falls short of that offered from the West, it is often more impressive, since it is swift and flexible, and interest rates on communist loans are only about two per cent compared with five to six per cent charged on loans from western countries'. (Nkrumah, *Neo-Colonialism*,

p. 243.) The Egyptian Government today would no doubt endorse this statement.

Since 1946 it has become customary to compare growth rates for different countries. While in the USSR this index has been taken as a pulse of the health of the country since 1928, since the last war the same criterion has been applied to a large number of countries.

Britain, too, has had problems with its growth rate, for while the 'national plan' originally laid down $4\frac{1}{2}$ per cent, only $2-2\frac{1}{2}$ per cent has been achieved so far. Whereas, for an underdeveloped country, the need is for new capital resources in order to lay the foundations of an economy, in the case of Britain the main problem has been to renew obsolete or old-fashioned capital equipment which, unlike that of Germany and Japan, has not had to be rebuilt from scratch, often with the aid of government, as a result of the last war.

Marx studied British capitalism in its early, competitive, phase, but he saw it dynamically, in the course of its development. The concentration of capital into the hands of gigantic businesses, and the accompanying technological progress, were both foreseen by him. But monopolistic tendencies, themselves emerging from competitive situations, put a brake on further technological development. '*The real barrier of capitalist production is capital itself,*' Marx wrote, so that 'while the capitalist mode of production is one of the historical means by which the material forces of production are developed and the world market required for them created, it is at the same time in continual conflict with this historical task and the conditions of social production corresponding to it'. (*Capital*, Vol. III, p. 293.)

So the growth and development of the economy under capitalism was fully recognised and studied by Marx. But because this system is orientated on 'making money', profit, surplus-value, capital to generate more capital, it is the profit motive and not social usefulness that is the motive force. But the increasing weight of constant against variable capital causes a general tendency for the rate of profit to fall even though counteracting tendencies are at work. As a result, we find that the large capital-intensive undertakings have increasingly to be state-supported or are in a monopolistic position in which they can make up their profits only through high price policies.

The irregularities of this system are natural to it, since there is no reason to expect anything but irregularity in a system in which thousands of decisions are taken independently of each other and there is no co-ordination apart from the dog-eat-dog process of the market. Hence, under capitalism, growth is punctuated by crises, whereas, said Marx, things could be different in a system 'in which the producers would regulate their production according to a preconceived plan'. (Ibid., pp. 306–7.)

In 1971 the export of capital from Britain reached over £600 million. Marx's comment on the role of foreign investment is highly pertinent here:

'If capital is sent to foreign countries, it is not done because there is absolutely no employment to be had for it at home. It is done because it can be employed at a higher rate of profit in a foreign country.' (Ibid., p. 300.)

The years 1970–2 have seen in Britain both a record level of unemployment since 1946, and a record investment of capital abroad. The illusions about 'full employment' have crumbled, and just at a time when the export of capital has reached a maximum. Yet it is admitted on all sides that capital investment at home is the essential prerequisite for economic growth.

Because of the sharpness of the contrast between the planned and unplanned economic systems, we are perhaps inclined to over-generalisation on both sides. In fact, there are considerable variations between countries within the capitalist system, and there are also variations between the countries which have planned economies. And not only does each country in each group differ from others in the same group; but each country today differs from what it was five or ten years ago.

A Soviet writer, T. Khachaturov (*Voprosii Ekonomikii*, No. 3, 1971), points out how the aims of planning change as development takes place. He writes that 'earlier, when many products were in short supply, we had to rely mainly on available resources, with due allowance for their planned increase'. But now it is becoming ever more expedient to start the planning calculations with demands and then go over to available resources'. The article stresses the aim, in Soviet planning today, to secure the 'maximum effect for given expenditures or minimum expenditures for a given effect'. But the effect has not got to be understood only statically, but as a process yielding immediate improvements in living standards and at the same time provision for future development. For this it becomes important 'not to restrict long-term planning by five-year periods alone' since 'large integrated long-term programmes of capital investment' require much longer. Moreover, more than one variant is possible, so that 'variant estimates' have to be worked out, suggesting alternative solutions.

At this point Khachaturov refers to 'bourgeois economics' as providing a useful concept in the 'production function', giving an indication of capital-labour effectiveness. While, to Marxists, 'capital certainly creates no output' because 'this is produced by manpower', the extent of productive efficiency is of major importance. 'Therefore, if the apologetic explanation of the role of capital in output is removed and the formula of the production function is translated into proper economic terms, it can be contended that the volume of output is predetermined by the number of employees engaged in material production and the productivity of their labour which depends in turn on the capital-employee ratio, the level of equipment, natural conditions, organisation of production, occupational skills and material and moral incentives for labour.' Among these latter he later enumerates 'better working and living conditions of workers and their higher cultural and ideological standards'.

Using the contemporary (and not Marx's) use of the term 'productive' and 'unproductive' labour, Khachaturov foresees a relative increase in services as the general process of economic growth continues. In future, 'the number of those engaged in the non-productive sphere will grow more quickly than in the sphere of material production'. He refers specially to trade, public catering and other services.

It should be noted that it is precisely this type of forecast, covering periods from five to twenty-five years or more, which is possible in planned economies but impossible under private enterprise. For the state that owns and controls the means of production is able to allocate them to their planned uses, so as to achieve targets which are determined in advance. In such a situation growth becomes planned growth, in which plans can be worked out which include estimated wants, estimated resources, and the optimum ways and means of making the resources supply the wants. In the case of wants, it is assumed that these will grow, within reason; and as regards resources, these are never regarded as being limited since new discoveries are always opening up new prospects.

On the other side, capitalist economies cannot be planned, although with Keynsian techniques they may be tinkered with from one year to the next. But while the USSR looks ahead to the fulfilment of its latest Five Year Plan, what can any capitalist state say with any authority today as to what will be the state of its economy in five years time?

The essential difference between socialism and capitalism is not that under socialism men can become independent of economic laws, but that they take control of them. As Engels said of the 'blind economic forces' of his day: 'So long as we obstinately refuse to understand their nature and their character—and the capitalist mode of production and its defenders set themselves against any such attempt—so long do these forces operate in spite of us, against us and so long do they control us. . . But once their nature is grasped, in the hands of the producers working in association they can be transformed from demoniac masters into willing servants.' (*Anti-Duhring*, p. 314.)

CHAPTER TEN

What Marx did not do

No survey of what Marx really did say on so many matters of economic importance in his day would be complete without summarising, at the risk of some repetition, what he did not say. Marx in his day was writing about the unsolved, and in his view insoluble, contradictions of capitalism; but the precise future course of development of the system was inevitably unknown to him although, in the last analysis, he saw its replacement by socialism and communism as the only logical way in which its basic contradictions could be solved.

We must not forget that in his lifetime Marx was not only working as a theoretical economist studying the laws of motion of capitalism. He was taking an active part in the working-class movement of his day; he was always faced with the stark bread-and-butter question of making both ends meet, and wrote many current political articles for this purpose; and he and his family were repeatedly saved from dire penury by the help of Frederick Engels who, as a result of his business activities, was able to make regular contributions to the Marx household finances. In addition, Marx suffered for years from ill-health, which added still further to his problems.

As a result, Marx's published work was in its nature 'unfinished'. Even Engels never succeeded in editing all of it. And Marx himself never enjoyed the luxury, available to most contemporary academic orthodox economists, of revising his work as a whole to present the world with an authentic 'authorised version' before his death.

There were some aspects of capitalist development and, still more, of the transition to a new state of society, which were not yet topical in Marx's day, and therefore did not receive full treatment. It has been the task of Marxists since Marx to develop these points, and but for some dogmatism engendered by the political environment, this work would have been tackled with considerably more flexibility than has been the case in practice. Today the outlook in this respect appears much more favourable.

What were the main points with which Marx did not deal, but which are highly relevant in the world today?

First, in his exposition of the Labour Theory of Value, Marx together with his contemporaries assumed competitive conditions. Under these conditions he showed how *labour-power* was bought by the employers, while *labour* was incorporated in the products. The excess of the labour supplied over the labour-power paid for provided the margin of surplus-value out of which profit, interest and rent had to come. Under competitive conditions there was a tendency for price to be pinned down in the direction of real value, and for profits to be equalised between firms.

Marx was far ahead of his orthodox contemporaries in that he perceived, what most orthodox economists do not perceive to this day, that successful competitors drive out or swallow up their less fortunate rivals so that, by consolidating their own successful businesses, they tend to grow from small competing firms into monopolists. This general tendency, for competition to give rise to monopoly, was established by Marx, has been confirmed by experience, but is still not yet recognised by orthodox economics.

But in dealing with the Labour Theory of Value and prices, Marx's analysis was confined to competitive conditions. At that time he still regarded monopoly as an 'accidental' influence on the market, and he never pursued the ramifications of the price system which would come about when monopolies played a dominant part in the economy and therefore the competitive tendencies to keep prices near to values, and to equalise profits, ceased to operate. This opens up an enormous field for Marxist study today which has still been far from adequately explored.

Today, in capitalist countries, inflation has become chronic. This is variously blamed on monetary factors, wage-demands, and the raising of prices; but in the world of the othodox there is no recognition that the role of monopoly in our economy is a basic cause.

To put it simply: If competitive capitalism tended to keep prices down—to 'marginal costs' in the orthodox terminology, or in the direction of 'values' in Marxist terms—then the super-cession of competition by monopoly means that the 'spontaneous' controls which operated during the phase of competitive capital-ism have ceased to exist. Rising prices are thus 'liberated' from the traditional competitive controls. 'Inflation' is simply another word for rising prices.

If inflation is seen as a reflection of monopoly-domination of the economic system, then it becomes clear that all the remedies which a Keynes or his disciples may put forward in the monetary and credit system cannot, in the long run, grapple with the problem.

This explanation of inflation may not, of course, be complete in every case. But it is an aspect which occurs to Marxists on the basis of Marx's original approach, while it remains in the main outside the ken of the orthodox and was not explored in detail by Marx himself.

This feature of capitalism did not yet come to the fore during the lifetime of either Marx or Engels. And it would appear, from much of their writing, that they were over-optimistic in assuming that socialist states would emerge in the countries of mature capitalism long before they have actually done so. They can be correctly criticised for underestimating the resilience of capital-ism (just as, incidentally, at least up to the beginning of the Nazi attack on the USSR in 1941, the Western world underestimated the resilience of socialism).

A second matter on which Marx would undoubtedly have spent more time, had he lived long enough, would have been the evolution of the monetary system towards the ever greater use of credit. For Marx, all money was essentially dependent on a

K

'money-commodity', gold. This, in his day, was unquestionably correct, but today Marxists are beginning to discuss whether the 'money-commodity' itself is not now being jettisoned.

In the recent discussion by Marxist economists in the USSR already mentioned (*supra*, pp. 100–1) an article has referred to 'paper gold' as taking the place of gold and to a recent trend in Soviet economic writing which recognises that 'gold itself has become a commodity with a monopoly price' so that more than one Soviet economist has now come to 'deny the role of gold as a measure of value in the conditions of present-day capitalism' despite the fact that Marx, in his own day, was quite explicit on this point. (Eidelnant, *loc. cit.*)

Atlas and Matyukhin, in their article (see p. 100), pointed out that nowadays 'one or several countries are capable to some degree of establishing control over internal monetary circulation and credit in other countries'. And the writers quote Lenin's reference to 'the change from the old type of capitalism, in which free competition predominated, to the new capitalism in which monopoly reigns'. They draw the conclusion that in this situation 'new forms of internal and international monetary circulation emerge'. However, these particular authors still hold the traditional Marxist view on the role of gold, and maintain that 'gold functions as a genuine, objectively valid, universal money', and the fact that the dollar is devalued in gold terms bears this out. There can be no doubt, however, that had Marx been alive today, he would have paid far more attention to the role of credit as a supplementary factor in economic life.

The third main field on which Marx was relatively silent, but which has now become a matter of major importance, was the way in which, and the rate at which, the transition from capitalism to socialism would be brought about.

In the days when they were writing, both Marx and Engels envisaged the maturing of the capitalist system, the maturing within it of the working class, and a transition in which the working people would take over state power. Whether this would be done by violent or Parliamentary means, in either case it would constitute a 'revolution', since it would mean the transfer of ownership of the means of production from private hands to public organisations. Never did Marx or Engels discuss the possibility that this might first come about, through a combination of particular political and economic circumstances, in a country which had not yet completed its development under capitalism; nor did they anticipate the sort of world situation which would arise if first one country, and then a group of countries, took the path to socialism while the rest of the world was still under capitalist and imperialist domination. Nor did they envisage the phenomenon of the so-called 'Third World' which is now a fact.

This does not mean, however, that Marx and Engels were unaware of the revolutionary potentialities of Russia. Both Engels and Marx paid attention to the Russian question during the 1870s, and Engels conducted a controversy with a Russian, P. N. Tchachov, during which he remarked that 'the overthrow of Russian tsardom, the dissolution of the Russian empire, . . . is . . . one of the first conditions for the final victory of the German proletariat. . .'

'The revolution which modern socialism strives to achieve is, briefly, the victory of the proletariat over the bourgeoisie, and the organisation of a new society by the destruction of all class differences.' He went on to examine the position of the peasantry in Russia, their relationship with the big landowners, 'artels' or co-operatives of hunters and workers, and the traditional communal ownership of land. While he criticised sharply what he regarded as Tchachov's naïve idea of revolution, he said with regard to the traditional communal ownership of the land that 'the possibility undeniably exists of transforming this social form into a higher one, if it should last until circumstances are ripe for that, and if it shows itself capable of development in such a way that the peasants no longer cultivate the land separately, but collectively; and to transform it into this higher form, without it being necessary for the Russian peasants to go through the intermediate stage of bourgeois small ownership. This, however, can only happen if, before the complete break-up of communal ownership, a proletarian revolution is successfully carried out in Western Europe.' (See *Marx, Selected Works*, Vol. II, London, pp. 669–85.) Engels concluded that Russia was 'on the eve of a revolution' but at that time did not see the Russian working class as yet strong enough to lead it.

Marx, a few years later, writing to Sorge on 27 September 1877, said of Russia: 'This time the revolution will begin in the East, hitherto the unbroken bulwark and reserve army of counter-revolution.' However, he, too, still only envisaged a 'bourgeois revolution' under the then existing conditions (Ibid., p. 669.) Moreover, in 1905, Lenin also still regarded the working class in Russia as not yet strong enough to lead the revolution forward to Socialism; but the development of the working class between 1905 and 1917 led him to change his view.

The Revolution of October 1917 occurred some 40 years after Marx and Engels were dealing with the Russian question. Much had changed, but the first socialist revolution still occurred in a country where capitalism had far from fully developed, and where the overwhelming majority of the population were still peasants. The new system therefore came into being in conditions not foreseen by Marx, and the 'two systems' have now existed in the world since 1917, a long period of co-existence also never envisaged by Marx and Engels.

If, then, we compare the world as it is today with what it was like when Marx and Engels were writing, we find that while their approach laid bare the development of capitalism, especially English capitalism, it did not explore in depth a number of implications of what they themselves wrote.

The inevitable evolution of monopoly from competition was made clear by Marx, but the study of value and prices in a monopoly-dominated capitalism was never undertaken by him. The continuous spread of the use of credit as a substitute for using the money-commodity, gold, was forecast in general by Marx, but its actual working was left to the future. Keynes' contribution, it might be said, has been a valiant attempt to utilise this same credit system so as to prolong the life of capitalism, while the essential foundation of its instability, the eternal contradiction between social production and private ownership, remains.

Therefore, to adopt Marx's method, and to follow up events from where he left off, using his method and applying it to the world as it is today, is to adopt a normal scientific procedure.

The capitalist system, for all the differences which exist between countries, is based on the private ownership of the means of production and production for private profit. The socialist system, again despite all differences, is based on the public ownership of the means of production and planned production for the present and future benefit of the community. In between these basic types lie the countries of the 'Third World'—a term usually applied to the 'underdeveloped' only—or countries with a 'mixed economy'—a term now sometimes applied even to capitalist Britain because some 40 per cent of the country's capital assets of all kinds are now publicly owned. But however 'mixed' the British economy may be said to be, it still preserves that shrine of private enterprise, the Stock Exchange. No country with a Stock Exchange can strictly be described as anything but capitalist.

It is clear that antagonism between these two social and economic systems can, at times, lead to war. Intervention against the Soviet Republic from 1918 to 1921; and the Nazi invasion from 1941 to 1945; intervention in China; intervention in Vietnam; and a host of other conflicts can be cited as clashes of the two rival social and economic systems and their ideologies. Equally, the Soviet interventions in Hungary and Czechoslovakia were part of the same picture, and it will remain a matter of controversy whether or not those interventions were strategically necessary measures to counter intervention on behalf of capitalism.

But there is also the possibility of coexistence without war. Both sides exist. And so far as they coexist without war, we have in fact got 'peaceful coexistence' between the two systems. This coexistence may simply be a state of antagonism stopping short of actual war. Or it may be fierce economic competition. Or it may be positive trade and co-operation in various fields. No study of Marxism today would be complete without some words on these problems about which, in his day, Marx never wrote.

CHAPTER ELEVEN

World Outlook: 'Convergence' or 'Coexistence'?

We have noted that during the lifetime of Marx it was assumed that the transition to a new socialist economic system would follow logically from the course of development in advanced capitalist countries. However, events decreed otherwise, and the Socialist Revolution was successful in Russia in 1917 while it failed in Germany one year later.

Hence there appeared on the agenda of history a number of new features which may be described as the 'capitalist encirclement' of the USSR from 1917 to 1945, and as the emergence of 'two world systems' from 1946 onwards.

Throughout the period since 1917 Marxists in the USSR have been very much aware of the antagonism of the surrounding imperialist states, a situation quite unforeseen by Marx and Engels. This had an adverse effect inside the USSR, making necessary the allocation of vast resources to defence which could have much more effectively been used for raising the standard of life more rapidly and for laying the foundations for even more rapid economic growth and development. At the same time it raised the issue of 'peaceful coexistence' of different social systems, as well as manifold speculations as to whether or not such coexistence of the two systems in fact meant their convergence.

Among the Marxists of Russia the idea of the possible necessity of existing on their own for a long time after their socialist revolution in a world in which imperialism continued was one which dawned only gradually. Already in August 1915 Lenin began to prepare the way for a possible socialist revolution in Russia *preceding* similar developments elsewhere. He then wrote: 'Uneven economic and political development is an absolute law of capitalism. Hence, the victory of socialism is possible, first in a few or even one capitalist country' which would then '*confront* the rest of the capitalist world.' (Lenin, *Collected Works*, Vol. 21, p. 342.)

Again, in November 1916, Lenin commented: 'And if the European proletariat cannot advance to socialism now . . . then East Europe and Asia can advance to democracy with seven-league strides only if tsarism is utterly smashed.' (Lenin, *Collected Works*, Vol. 23, p. 133.) And when, in the revolutionary year 1917, the workers, peasants and soldiers were organising their own elected councils (soviets), Lenin saw the significance of this and the possibility of Soviet power as a new form of socialist state to replace not only the relics of tsarism but the unstable 'Provisional Government' which the property owners were still hoping would save capitalism in Russia.

Internationally, Lenin realised that the Soviet State would have to exist for a time in a world dominated by capitalist states. At the Second Congress of Soviets on November 8, 1917, he therefore came out in favour of treaties with such states, but on certain conditions: 'We reject all clauses based on plunder and violence, but we shall welcome all clauses containing provisions for good-neighbourly relations and economic agreements, these we shall not reject'.

In 1919, in a letter to the workers of the USA, he offered them, 'after peace is concluded, not only resumption of trade relations but also the possibility of receiving concessions in Russia . . . A durable peace would bring such relief to the working people of Russia that they would undoubtedly agree to certain concessions being granted'. (Lenin, *Letter to American Workers*, 23 September 1919.) And, a few weeks later, he told the *Chicago Daily News* (5 October 1919): 'We are decidedly for an economic understanding with America, with all countries but *especially* with America'. And to the *New York Evening Journal* (18 February 1920) he spoke of 'peaceful coexistence with all peoples.

'Let the American capitalists leave us alone. We shall not touch them. We are even ready to pay them in gold for any machines, tools, etc., useful to our transport and industries.'

And so a policy of trade, based on peaceful coexistence, was launched from the very first days of the Soviet system.

On the other side, however, great obstacles were placed in the way of such trade. In Britain, while some voices were raised in Parliament, the business world and the press for entry into the post-revolutionary Russian market, on the other hand there was strong opposition, partly for undisguised political reasons, and partly on the ground—later proved completely false—that trade with Soviet Russia was a bad risk.

But many businessmen, the trade unions, and even the government were moving towards the normalising of trade relations, and the Allied Supreme Council at San Remo on 25 April 1920, authorised a meeting with a Soviet delegation to 'take all steps necessary to secure the development of trade relations between Russia and the Allied countries'. In May 1920, negotiations began for a British-Soviet Trade Agreement, and this was finally signed in March 1921.

It is not relevant here to survey the ups and downs of trade between the USSR on the one hand and Britain, the USA and other capitalist countries on the other. Suffice it to say that there have been many such ups and downs, and political rather than economic reasons have been responsible for this. But nevertheless, Soviet trade with the rest of the world has increased at the same time as the internal economy has developed, and far from such development leading to autarcky and isolation, it has on the contrary led to a growth of exchange between the USSR and other countries.

In the orthodox tradition of teaching Economics, foreign trade has usually occupied a special position because, as Cairncross puts it, 'countries are more than geographical areas; they are areas with economic systems of their own, cut off by political frontiers from the economic systems of their neighbours. They have, as a rule, their own currency and their own banking system. Their commodity markets are hedged about with customs duties and customs officers. Their capital-market is partially insulated. . . Their labour market is protected against immigration. . . Above all, each country has its own government'. (Cairncross, op. cit., p. 198.)

While Cairncross writes that countries have 'economic systems of their own' he nevertheless, in his discussion of international trade, concentrates overwhelmingly on those countries which have varying versions of the capitalist economic system. He pays little attention to that part of world trade, a growing part, which is conducted with and by the countries with planned economies. For it is still traditional in orthodox economics to consider international trade on the basis of a theory rooted in the abstraction of perfect competition, and then, starting from this, to consider the realities of trade relations between capitalist countries. Even then, little attention is paid to the complications which arise through large capital movements as a result of which decisive enterprises in one country become the private property of investors in another.

While the tendency to ignore trade with the socialist countries is predominant in orthodox economics textbooks, it should be mentioned that there is a wide range of opinion on the matter. For example, Lord Balogh chides Professor Jacob Viner because the latter 'refuses to consider the problem of trade relations between the USSR and individualistic economic systems—surely the most urgent of the problems before us'. (Balogh, op. cit., p. 213.) The difference, in effect, between the two views is that, consciously or unconsciously, Viner was reflecting the official State Department view at the time, whereas Balogh reflected the view of those British businessmen and others who could see nothing but advantage to Britain from developing trading relations with the planned economy countries.

The basic traditional theoretical principle underlying foreign trade which is still enunciated by the orthodox is the so-called

'law' or 'principle' of Comparative Advantage. This is a theoretical rationalisation of Free Trade on the ground that, given
freedom of competition both within and between countries, every
country will then—other things being equal—export those goods
in the production of which it enjoys the greater comparative
advantage in exchange for those goods in which it has less comparative advantage or greater comparative disadvantage. This
basic position would then mean that every country would export
those goods it was in the best position to spare in exchange for
goods in which it was in relatively the greatest need.

But this principle is, in reality, so highly vulnerable, that
nowadays under capitalism it has mainly historical interest.
Almost all orthodox economists recognise that protective tariffs
are economically justified in a number of specific situations
which, taken together, give a far more realistic picture of the
world situation than any theory of perfect competition: Protection
is justified (a) when strategic reasons take priority over purely
economic ones, (b) when an 'infant' industry is in danger of being
undercut by more developed foreign firms during its period of
growth to maturity, (c) when protection is necessary against
'unfair' competition from abroad, that is, when foreign goods are
being offered excessively cheaply. This can happen in any case
when a foreign monopoly is 'dumping' surplus stocks abroad
below cost, thus 'unfairly' undercutting the producers in the
receiving country. It can also happen when a country permits
sweated labour in certain of its industries, thus giving them an
'artificial' comparative advantage in the export market.

Yet another measure which has received world publicity
recently is the procedure of using a general tariff to protect the
currency reserves of a country, as for example the 10 per cent
import surcharge imposed by President Nixon in the USA as a
device to cut down imports and thus improve the balance of
trade.

When all these exceptions to freedom of trade are taken
together, and we recognise the fact that competition both within
and between countries is nowadays interlaced with monopolistic

and semi-monopolistic practices at all levels, we find that while lip-service is still paid to the reduction of tariffs; in fact they continue to be operated by all capitalist countries, always for one or more of the above 'accepted' reasons.

While this is the situation in the capitalist world, no attention is paid by the orthodox to what happens in the countries with planned economies, in all of which there is a state monopoly of foreign trade.

Here there is no assumption of a competition which does not exist, but a realistic appraisal of each country's needs under the plan, and of each country's relative surpluses. In considering what goods a country can afford to export, or to produce for export, and what it should import at any particular time, the planning authorities are, in fact, weighing up the comparative advantages and disadvantages of producing particular goods at home, or whether it is worth while to import them from abroad in exchange for some home-produced product. In general terms, therefore, we may say that under state planning an attempt is made consciously to assess a country's balance of advantages and disadvantages so as to import the maximum of utility for the country at the cost of exporting (or sacrificing) a minimum of utility. In essence, this is what the principle of comparative advantage is all about.

In the countries of planned economy, of course, one year's foreign trade is not considered in isolation. The plan provides for growth and development, and it is therefore impossible to have any static yardstick for comparative advantages and disadvantages. It may be necessary, for development, to forego imports of certain consumers' goods for example, in order that stocks of means of production may be built up.

It is also necessary, if estimates of projected exports and imports are to be correctly balanced, that the domestic system of costing be as accurate as possible, because in so far as the costing system is faulty, serious errors may result in the choice of exports to pay for particular imports.

Again, in the planned economies, strategic and political aims are taken into account, so that judgements on foreign trade may not be entirely based on economic considerations. While, for example, the Soviet Ministry of Foreign Trade acts mainly to secure economic agreements on the basis of *economic* advantage, there is no doubt that in some cases, such as the undertaking to absorb Cuba's sugar surplus over a number of years, political motives are paramount in reaching an economic decision.

Finally, it must be recognised that once a state monopoly of foreign trade has been established, there is a possibility of manoeuvre in dealing with any one customer or any one product which is not enjoyed by the small private firm. Just as ICI or Unilever in their international relations enjoy enormous bargaining power because of their scale of operation, so, too, any Ministry of Foreign Trade of any socialist country also enjoys such powers of manoeuvre because of the scale on which it operates.

Moreover, since the respective Ministries of Foreign Trade handle all the goods coming into and going out of a country, and since foreign exchange is kept purely for foreign trading purposes, the Ministries are able to plan their trade much more in terms of actual goods than is the case with capitalist countries dependent on free movements of foreign exchange, subject to varying degrees of influence by the respective central banks. The *Economist* underlined this aspect of the matter on 27 November 1971 when it wrote 'that east-west trade is in many ways a relatively sophisticated form of international barter rather than the result of an international market'.

Even more, of course, is this so among the socialist countries themselves which, within COMECON, are now jointly planning various aspects of their trade and production so that more and more agreements are coming into operation for joint exploitation of resources, for specialisation between countries according to their particular facilities, and co-operation in developing enterprises for their common benefit such as an International Investment Bank, the Friendship Oil Pipe Line and a large range of less spectacular items.

While the existing socialist governments have all come into existence in different situations, with different national backgrounds, it is a deliberate aim to co-ordinate their development so that ultimately their standards of living will be brought together so that there will be no advanced and no underdeveloped countries among them. They will, as Khrushchev once said, 'all enter Communism together'.

In the general process of increasing trade and economic relations between the socialist and capitalist states there has been a steady growth in the interchange of visits, whether for purposes of trade, tourism, or the exchange of specialised information and knowledge. While in the socialist countries such exchanges are regarded as part of 'coexistence' which does not affect the essential difference between the two systems, there have been many in the West who have identified these tendencies with the 'convergence' of the two systems. Both the USSR and USA, for example, may be described as 'industrial' societies, since in both there is a development of industry while the specific weight of agriculture in the total economy is declining. Some of the exponents of the convergence theory deny that the socialist countries are 'socialist' at all; while others take the view that capitalism is itself approximating to socialism. We may consider a few examples.

One of those who has done most, perhaps, to minimise the differences between the USSR and capitalist countries is Professor Herbert Marcuse, 'whose teaching', says his publisher, 'gives inspiration to the international student protest movement.' (Marcuse, *Soviet Marxism*, Pelican, p. 1.)

In so far as Marcuse deals with economics at all in this book, it is to assert, repeatedly and without evidence, that 'individuals can be free only if they themselves control production' and to imply that this does not happen in the USSR. Therefore, he says, the USSR 'does not have a *raison d'être* essentially different from that of capitalist society'. (Op. cit., p. 83.) He finds that 'the very antagonisms which it strives to overcome' exist in the 'contrast between the level of productivity and the level of consumption' and 'the conflict between social and individual needs'.

(Ibid., p. 84.) Yet a reference back to what Marx himself envisaged in the first stage of communist society, as it emerges from capitalism, makes it clear that he never envisaged that the whole social product would be turned over to the population for consumption. He enumerated a number of 'deductions' which, with defence added, make up in fact the very 'antagonisms' listed by Marcuse. (See *supra*, p. 66.)

Again, Marcuse requires that in the USSR 'production and the production relations' be 'reorganised in such a way that the rise of the level of material and intellectual culture is not the mere by-product but the goal of the social effort'. (Ibid., p. 85.) But it is precisely this goal of the USSR that is specifically stated in its Constitution (Article II) as being that of 'increasing the public wealth, of steadily raising the material and cultural standards of the working people.' At the most, Marcuse could argue that, so far, the allocation of resources to economic growth has been excessive, or that distribution of the consumable portion has been too favourable to the administrative personnel. These are simply matters of degree, on the deciding of priorities, but not of the principle of planning of such. Personal differences of view on such questions are inevitable. It is only to be noted that, since Marcuse wrote his criticism, the emphasis in the USSR has shifted more in favour of the production of consumers' goods; and more attention has been paid to raising the incomes of the lowest paid. The possibilities in this field are always limited by the degree of security or insecurity in the international situation.

As to Marcuse's identification of 'freedom' with 'control of production', and stress on the need to 'bring the administration under direct popular control' (ibid., p. 155), a great deal depends on what meaning is read into these words. For it has always been a tenet of Marxism that some form of democratic control over administrators is desirable, and in the USSR, despite central planning, repeated attempts have been made to make such control a reality. Among those operative at present are the obligation of all factory managers to report regularly to 'Production Conferences' on their conduct of their responsibilities. This is combined with trade union control over hiring and firing. And in cases where factory managers treat their subordinates either illegally or inconsiderately, it is quite possible for the union on the job to secure the dismissal of such a manager. In this, of course, variations occur according to personalities involved, and the Soviet press has from time to time published articles criticising the trade unions for not being sufficiently vigilant in defending their members' interests.

At the same time, a planned economy demands, for efficiency, a certain amount of centralisation. Moreover, there is no ideal balance between centralised leadership and control and 'initiative from below'. This balance is something which must inevitably vary from situation to situation and from time to time. Nobody today, for example, would dispute the fact that in the last years of Stalin centralisation was carried to fantastic extremes, supported by the illegal activities of the state security services. At the other extreme, everyone today has become convinced that Khrushchev's 'decentralisation' measure of setting up Regional Economic Councils led to a degree of local autonomy which also did not serve the best interests of the economy as a whole. On this issue, then, there is no 'final' answer, and the system of planning does not stand or fall by the exact balance, achieved at any particular time, between centralisation and democracy.

While, in most of his book, Marcuse is denying that the Soviet system basically differs from capitalism, and therefore provides many of the arguments frequently used to justify the claim that the two systems are converging, he at one point appears to foresee for the USSR a prospect which is entirely consistent with Marx's own long-term perspective. Marcuse at this point writes:

'Unless another world war, or similar catastrophe occurs which would change the situation, the direction is towards a growing welfare state. Rising standards of living up to a practically free distribution of basic goods and services, steadily extending mechanisation of labour, exchangeability of technical functions, expanding popular culture—these developments constitute the probable trend. It is likely to lead to the gradual assimilation of urban and agricultural, intellectual and physical labour . . . Technical progress will overtake the repressive restrictions imposed at earlier stages' leading to 'a reduction of the gap between the top strata and the underlying population. . . Personal rule will increasingly be replaced by collective administration.' (Ibid., pp. 154–5.)

In these phrases, at least, if not in many others, Marcuse sees the likely development of the USSR to be precisely along the lines foreseen by Marx and Engels. It therefore remains a mystery how a perspective which includes 'rising living standards' leading to 'a practically free distribution of basic goods and services' can in any way whatsoever be identified with capitalism. Yet in the same book Marcuse tries to make out that the USSR 'does not have a *raison d'être* essentially different from that of capitalist society'. In his few words on the future perspective he makes clear that a different *raison d'être* definitely exists.

Another writer, the American, Paul Mattick, should be mentioned here as also maintaining the view that socialism does not exist in the countries of planned economy. His publishers claim for him a 'grasp of both Marxist and Keynsian theory'. In his *Marx & Keynes*, Mattick goes to great lengths to divorce the countries with planned economies from both Marx and Socialism. What is left, it seems, may be called the result of 'state-capitalist', 'state-socialist', or 'Keynsian revolutions'. (Op. cit., p. 278.) A wide terminology is provided to choose from, so long as the words Marxist and Socialist are not used.

Mattick without justification attacks Joan Robinson for suggesting that the Labour Theory of Value may come into its own under Socialism. (See *supra*, pp. 113–4.) And he attacks the Socialist countries for what he calls 'the development of capital production in the name of "socialism" or "communism"', calling this 'a paradox too farfetched to have entered Marx's mind'. (Ibid., p. 279.)

This statement is obscure, to say the least.

If, of course, by capital, we mean privately owned capital used to employ labour for profit, there is no 'development of capital

L

production' in the socialist countries, and the comment is without meaning.

If, alternatively, by 'capital production' Mettick refers to the production of 'capital goods' or 'means of production', then, as we have already seen, Marx certainly did regard this as essential under socialism, and he provided for one of the main 'deductions' from the national product, before distribution to the population for consumption, to be precisely this provision for the future. In this case, Marx did provide for just the sort of provision of means of production which is regarded as a first priority in all the socialist countries. Therefore the suggestion that the socialist countries are not Marxist in this respect is simply unfounded.

A further statement by Mattick is that the countries which call themselves Socialist, and Marxist, still 'retain the capitalistic division of the conditions of production between workers and non-workers'. (Ibid., p. 321.) How this is substantiated is again not clear, and as the countries concerned have practically eliminated 'unearned income', so that all incomes are earnings, or pensions, or student grants, or family allowances, it is quite impossible to see what is meant by referring to the retention of the 'capitalistic division . . . between workers and non-workers'.

Finally, to label the revolutions in all the socialist countries as 'Keynsian' rather than 'state-capitalist' or 'state-socialist' is more mystifying than ever. Whatever 'revolution' Keynes propounded, it was above all a 'revolution' based on the private ownership of the means of production, however much state interference might be introduced. The revolutions of the socialist countries all centre, however, on the ending of private ownership of the main means of production and the institution of public ownership, through the state, the local authorities, and co-operatives. To refuse to see this difference of principle naturally leads to inability to distinguish between capitalism and socialism and to the identifying of the two systems, to a form of 'convergence' based on the negation of the socialist nature of the socialist countries.

While Marcuse and Mattick approach the socialist countries as if to deny their socialism, and thus to identify the basic difference between the social systems, Professor Galbraith approaches the subject from the opposite side, implying, in fact, that capitalism is moving towards the same sort of planning as socialism. Here, too, however, we find that the reasons given do not bear close examination. The case is maintained only by refusing to observe the difference which results from the change in ownership of the means of production.

As Galbraith correctly points out, both the USA and USSR are countries which are developing industrially. On this basis of fact, he proceeds to maintain, first, that 'the Soviet resolution of the problem of authority in the industrial enterprise is not unlike that in the west—although no one can be precisely sure. Full social authority over the large enterprise is proclaimed. Like that of the stockholder and the Board of Directors in the United States, it is celebrated in all public ritual. The people and Party are paramount. But in practice large and increasing autonomy is accorded to the enterprise'. (Op. cit., Pelican edn, p. 115.)

So what?—While the degree to which American shareholders or Soviet workers and citizens actually exercise control over their directors may vary greatly from place to place and time to time, the essential difference still remains: capitalist directors are responsible to their shareholders who are the owners of the capital, and on whose behalf the directors run the business in order to make a profit, whether it is all distributed in dividends or ploughed back into the business. Soviet managers are responsible both to society as a whole, embodied in the Ministry to which they are responsible; and to those working under them, to whom they must regularly render account of their stewardship. The effectiveness of these procedures may certainly vary, but the procedures are there, and they are fundamentally different in the two systems.

On planning, Galbraith says that 'the firm is the basic planning unit in the western economies. In the Soviet system it is still the state'. (Ibid., p. 113.) This is true as far as it goes, but it would have been a more complete formula if it had said the *privately-owned* firm *run for profit* is the basic planning unit in the west; while all planning units in the USSR, from the Planning Department of a factory to the State Planning Commission of the country as a whole, operate *publicly owned enterprises* for the *common good*, in so far as this can be correctly ascertained.

With these totally different approaches to planning, it is surprising to find that Galbraith, some pages later, says that 'both systems are subject to the imperatives of industrialisation. This for both means planning'. (Ibid., p. 335.) And earlier, while he recognises that there 'is no tendency for the Soviet and the Western systems to convergence by the return of the former to the market,' thus exploding one popular myth, he goes on to say that 'there is measurable convergence to the same form of planning'. (Ibid., p. 116.)

Later in the book he throws all caution to the winds and declares that 'convergence between the two ostensibly different industrial systems occurs on all fundamental points'. (Ibid., p. 391.) Apart from some rather rude comments on Marx and his followers he at least draws from his wrong assessment the wise conclusion that peaceful coexistence is both possible and desirable.

Galbraith's facile idea of 'convergence' (reached by ignoring the basic differences) is to be rejected, but his words on coexistence should be taken to heart. He opposes the view 'that the arms competition is ultimately benign' (Ibid., p. 335) and advocates 'agreement on arresting and eliminating the competition in lethal technology' as being 'much less painful if competition continues and is encouraged and widened in non-lethal spheres.' (Ibid., pp. 344–5.) In this, his views coincide with those of Marxists, as also does the main theme of his novel *The Triumph*.

Whatever the changes which have taken place in capitalism since Marx died, or in socialism in Russia since 1917, the fundamental difference between the two economic systems remains. In the capitalist world since 1917 technology has developed enormously, and on this basis the workers in the developed capitalist countries have enjoyed some of the crumbs. Nationalisation, and at least lip-service to 'planning', have spread in the west, not uninfluenced by what has happened in the socialist countries. But some nationalisation and some 'planning' do not affect the fundamental social and economic structure based on private ownership.

A study of developments in the capitalist world since 1917 show a vast further concentration of capital, now reaching international proportions, so that, while governments may still be nominally independent, foreign ownership of the means of production on their territories is increasing. If present tendencies continue, the manufacturing industry of Britain will by the 1980s probably be predominantly foreign-owned, and therefore the policies of companies in this country will be decided by Boards of Directors acting on behalf of 'international capital'.*

It is at this stage of world development that Professor Galbraith sees more 'planning'. But this is planning by international and national privately-owned companies which are often making use of states for the further increase of their profits and their capital.

On the Soviet side, much also has changed since 1917. A backward mainly agricultural country has become the world's second

---

* In Britain today, large companies like Shell Transport, British Petroleum, ICI, Unilever, British-American Tobacco and Courtaulds among our top ten, all have extensive international ramifications. In 1970 a 'marriage' was being discussed, though it did not come off, between ICI and Courtaulds, which *The Economist* (10 January 1970) described as 'by far the biggest merger in British industrial history, creating a giant worth nearly £2,000 million worth of capital employed'. Even if the negotiations were at that time abortive, the tendency, innate in capitalism, is clear. As far as international ramifications are concerned, Unilever trades in some 63 countries and controls some five or six hundred firms—a considerable number of which continue to trade under their old independent names thus giving a false picture of competition. Barclays DCO holds banking assets of nearly £2,000 million and operates in more than 40 countries. In Britain itself US investment has risen from £300 million in 1950 to over £2,500 million today. The concentration of capital both within and between countries is now increasingly being studied. Orthodox economists are investigating facts which, in principle, Marx forecast more than 100 years ago while his orthodox contemporaries either turned a blind eye or suffered from a blind spot. See also *Postscript*, p. 171.

most important industrial one. In the course of development the techniques of planning have also developed. The First Five Year Plan made many broad estimates that had later to be modified. But nevertheless, the Soviet growth rate remains ahead of those of the capitalist countries, Japan has been the only known exception to this.

With the growth in the scale of the Soviet economy; and with the growing co-ordination of the plans of the socialist countries; some degree of decentralising inside the USSR has proved essential. At the same time, with the rise in productive capacity, so the resources have grown for supplying the needs of consumers. In the First Five Year Plan as well as during the postwar period of reconstruction, stress was laid mainly on quantity of production. But now quality is being increasingly stressed and the consumer's 'veto' on bad products becomes increasingly effective as choice is increased. By insisting that factories must effectively *sell* their products, and not simply be credited with *production* figures, there is now a new stimulus to ensure the quality of the consumer's goods produced.

While stress is laid on 'profitability' in the USSR, it should always be remembered that the only legitimate way in which a Soviet enterprise can increase its profit is by greater efficiency of production, not by cutting wages or raising prices. A direct link has thus been established between increasing productivity and increasing production in the USSR; a link which is often absent from increases in productivity in Britain. In other words: In the USSR increased productivity is passed on to the consumer in increased output and lower prices. Under capitalism it frequently means increased output per head, redundancy, and no increase in output at all.

As viewed by Soviet Marxists, relations between the socialist countries and the 'West' can be broken down into 'peaceful co-existence' on the one hand—which may be described as simultaneous existence on this planet without war—and 'co-operation and competition' on the other. Each side at any time can gain by exporting to, and importing from, the other. At the same time each side, starting from its own current level, is interested in growth and development. For planning such development, the planned economies obviously enjoy an advantage, since the public authorities own and control the resources whose utilisation they are planning. Equally, under a planned economy the state's monopoly of foreign trade provides the advantages of scale, diversification and manoeuvrability, just as large companies, under capitalism, enjoy such advantages as compared with their smaller rivals. In bargaining with Ministries of Foreign Trade in socialist countries, private firms clearly stand to gain by size, and if necessary by forming consortia to enable them to negotiate on an equal level with Ministries which, by the very nature of their work, are equipped for large-scale negotiations.

Despite the wartime alliance that had brought together Churchill, Roosevelt and Stalin, the Cold War was launched in 1947 and lasted nearly twenty-five years before President Nixon made a decisive turn in his relations with the Communist countries. Now, it does appear that some consolidation of peaceful coexistence may become possible, which will undoubtedly mean more 'east-west trade', more exchanges of technical information, and possibly more co-operation in such projects as space research, the protection of the world's fish resources and the combating of pollution in all its forms, including nuclear explosions. But the two social and economic systems will continue, on the basis of their own momentum, and there is no evidence that co-operation between them in specific fields will in any way affect the structure of property ownership within either system.

So just as the Political Economy of Marxism will continue, though of course taking account of changes in capitalism and the new problems raised by socialism; so too will the orthodox tradition in economics continue so long as there are economists who accept as essential facts of life the private ownership of the means of production and production for profit.

Long ago Lenin posed the problem of 'who will defeat whom?' This problem is not yet answered. History will decide. And it may still take a long time to make its verdict clear.

CHAPTER TWELVE

Conclusion

The aim of this book has been to demonstrate to students of orthodox economics that there is an alternative system of economic thought which has been greatly underrated, neglected, and actively misrepresented. In spite of all that has been said against it, and in spite of the extent to which it has been simply ignored, Marxist Political Economy in its day revealed tendencies in capitalism which nobody in the orthodox camp would then recognise; and even today, although events confirm the forecasts of Marx in many striking respects, it is still fashionable to write him off as old-fashioned and 'exploded'.

The two fundamental approaches to economics are, firstly, the orthodox one based on the acceptance, as given, of the private ownership of the means of production, and production for private profit. Used in this sense, it should be noted that private owner-ship includes ownership by 'public' companies in the British legal sense. Accepting private ownership as fundamental, the private supply of the factors of production is treated as inevitable, and, naturally enough, the resulting economic theories are likely to be acceptable to all who find the system of private enterprise congenial.

The other, Marxist, approach is based on the historical fact that capitalism is a stage in economic evolution and therefore, as a result of this fact alone, there is no reason to presume that it is eternal. Moreover, if economic problems are approached from the standpoint of those who have to live by selling their labour-power, having nothing else to sell, they are likely to be seen in a rather different light from the view of the businessman or landlord regarding the same problems.

One of the USA's greatest writers, Jack London, who was himself an adherent of Marxism, put the situation into the musings of one of his characters as follows:

'Work, legitimate work, was the source of all wealth. Whether it was a sack of potatoes, a grand piano or a seven-passenger touring car, it came into being only by a performance of work. Where the bunce came in was in the distribution of these things after labour had created them. By hundreds of thousands, men sat up and schemed how they could get between the workers and the things the workers produced. These schemers were business men. The size of the whack they took was determined by no rule of equity, but by their own strength and swinishness. It was always a case of 'all the traffic could bear'. (London, *Burning Daylight*.)

The thoughts expressed above are as natural and as reasonable for a wage-earner as are the following thoughts which Marx attributes to a capitalist: 'His profit of enterprise appears to him as independent of the ownership of capital, it seems to be the result of his function as a non-proprietor—*a labourer*.' (*Capital*, Vol. III, pp. 446–7.)

If we now take these two different but both reasonable approaches, coming from representatives of two distinct classes, and build up a 'scientific' system of Political Economy or Economics based on each of the two approaches, we emerge with Marxist Political Economy in the first case and orthodox capitalist Economics in the second.

It is one of the first aims of this book to show that both approaches are scientific, each on its own premises.

The wage-earner, however much he may be indoctrinated to the contrary by the capitalist mass media, knows *from experience* that it is labour that produces wealth. This, as Marx has shown, conforms to the whole historical experience of the evolution of production, but is disguised by the forms and procedures of capitalism. On the other hand, the property-owner, the capitalist, *knows* that without *his* factory no production would take place. And therefore he regards his factory, as much as the workers in it, as 'creating' wealth. But how did the factory ever become his? And here Marx gives an exhaustive picture of the historical emergence, by a process of slavery, enclosures and expropriations, of the system of private ownership. He shows that there is nothing 'natural' about this, but that it is something which evolved over a long and violent period of social history.

Thus, starting out with the historical fact that it was man's effort—labour—that gave 'value' to the 'free' gifts of nature by working on them to give them use-value or utility, Marx examined the process by which all value can be reduced to 'socially necessary labour' of 'average' quality. And similarly, labour-power itself has a value, the socially necessary labour to keep up *its* supply. But this, as Marx clearly points out, is itself the product of tradition and custom and trade union organisation. It is therefore not something static, but changing with circumstances.

The source of 'profit' lies basically in the difference between what is paid for labour-power on the one hand, and the value actually produced by that labour on the other. It is in this difference that lies the phenomenon of 'exploitation' which is characteristic of capitalism. Marx made clear that exploitation, as such, had existed in earlier societies as well, exemplified by both slavery and serfdom, but it is capitalist exploitation which he examined in the greatest detail, endeavouring to reveal its nature where orthodoxy tended to obscure it.

Capitalism, in its striving for profit, always tends to try to keep down the living standards of the workers, and hence Marx has been credited with a 'law' of 'increasing poverty'. But he also drew attention to counteracting tendencies, including the rise in productivity resulting from technological progress and rises in wages due to trade union organisation. Moreover, while in his day the increasing of the working day was extensively used to get more out of the workers, both trade unionism and the law today, with stricter limitations on working hours and overtime, make this possibility less available than it once was.

Marx laid stress on the tendency of the rate of profit to fall; but this cannot be mechanically proved or disproved by simple reference to company dividends. Marx's thesis was that since surplus value is derived from the exploitation of labour, and since the general tendency is for the 'organic composition of capital' to take the form of ever more 'constant' capital in proportion to the 'variable' capital spent on employing labour, so a less and less proportion of total capital is spent in a way which brings in surplus-value, the source of profit.

It is this which gives rise to the tendency for the rate of profit to fall; but a number of counteracting tendencies may operate to offset this tendency. The fall in the cost of constant capital is one of these, as also a number of 'accidental' factors such as monopoly —which has become of predominant importance since the time when Marx wrote. In practice, today, it is hard to disentangle the extent to which the rate of profit in Marx's sense has actually fallen while, because of monopolistic price policies, firms have been able to recoup themselves for this by selling goods at prices far about their 'values' as compared to what would have happened with similar costs under competitive conditions.

What does seem clear from a survey of capital-intensive production is that, without actual state support in the form of subsidies (which are levied on other sectors of the economy) or without near-monopolistic price policies, such enterprises under present-day capitalism would not be viable. This would confirm the general line of Marx's argument.

Marx saw surplus value as the real source of profit, rent, and interest. But he also recognised that, as between the capitalists themselves, there could be a great many transactions, profitable to one and unprofitable to another, which did not involve production at all. While he foresaw, with the development of credit, a growth of these non-productive activities under capitalism, he never went into any detailed examination of the extent to which they would spread in the phase of monopoly domination of the system. To Marx, profits which arose for one group of capitalists at the expense of another were simply redistributions of surplus value among the capitalist class as a whole and were not to be confused with the origin of surplus value as such.

It seems that much that has been written in criticism of the Labour Theory of Value and of the Falling Rate of Profit loses weight when considered against Marx's actual formulations and the qualifications which he himself made. When Professor Joan Robinson writes that 'no point of substance in Marx's argument depends upon the labour theory of value' (Robinson, *Essay on Marxian Economics*, p. 22) she is surely throwing out the baby with the bathwater because, especially at the present stage of capitalism, the Labour Theory of Value gives no guide to *prices* as they are, though in theory it can still give sound guidance as to what they *ought to be* in a rationally organised society. Again, in dismissing the theory of the falling rate of profit as unsound, it appears that she is looking at book-keeping profits as they are, without examining the extent to which, in each case, these profits are really forthcoming at the point of production as surplus-value, or are simply derived from the charging of monopolistic prices on the market. The extent to which prices in the modern world deviate from values is far greater than under competitive capitalism, and this deviation is one of the main means by which companies offset their own experience of the falling rate of profit in the Marxist sense. The important contribution which Joan Robinson has made in introducing Marx to the orthodox lies above all in her recognition, with Marx, that '*owning* capital is not a productive activity'. (Ibid., p. 18.) But once this is accepted, then the Labour Theory of Value of necessity follows. But this does not mean that value must be equated with price, especially nowadays.

One of the misleading myths which has been spread about Marxism is that it in some way is connected with equality of incomes. This may well have arisen as a result of Marx's emphasis on the need to put an end to 'unearned' incomes, so that all incomes should arise from productive work. But beyond this

Marx did not go, recognising that the details of distribution on the basis of work done were something to be determined by society when it was confronted with the practical problems involved.

At a time when all orthodox economists accepted competition as the essence of capitalism, with monopoly as a rare exception, Marx pointed to the inevitability of the concentration of capital in fewer and fewer hands as a result of successful competition itself. Thus competition inevitably would give rise to monopoly. So, today, while orthodox economists still write about competitive enterprise as if this were the foundation of contemporary capitalism, Marxists are writing about the 'monopoly capitalism' which Marx foresaw, as now having become the dominant feature of the system. It is true, however, that even with monopoly dominant smaller firms still compete, and the large monopolies themselves compete against each other, negotiate, and at times swallow one another up.

The conception of a 'general crisis of capitalism' is a central idea of Marxists, since they regard crisis as endemic to the system. There have repeatedly been periods when Marx has been declared 'out of date', because of a 'Ford miracle', 'full employment', the West German or Japanese 'miracles'. Yet such 'miracles' and 'refutations' of Marxism have proved to have been but temporary, though a general rise in welfare and affluence must be acknowledged, and is indeed in accord with Marx's own comments on the effect on the workers' living standards which would result from growing productivity. Despite growing productivity, the crisis atmosphere continues, and the devaluation of the all-mighty dollar is but the latest symptom.

Paul Mattick, though he has some very ill-chosen comments to make on the socialist countries in his *Marx and Keynes*, pays an interesting tribute to Marx as a theoretician. He writes that 'however limited his theory may be, due to its high level of abstraction, it is the only theory of capitalist accumulation which has found verification in the actual course of capitalism's development. Whether we consider the rising organic composition of capital; the tendentially falling rate of profit as actualised in the capitalistic crisis; the increasing severity of crises; the production of an industrial reserve army; the unrelieved misery of the great bulk of the world's population despite increasing wealth as capital; the elimination of competition through competition (or concentration, centralisation, and monopolisation of capital)—we cannot fail to notice the pattern of development projected by Marx'. (Op. cit., p. 191.)

Unlike Marx, Marxists today are less prone to expect the imminent collapse of capitalism. It is today recognised that events move more slowly, and that capitalism as a system, though losing ground on a world scale, has proved to be more viable than Marx in his day imagined possible. But the symptoms of crisis are ever with us, though symptoms may be treated successfully for quite a time without eliminating their basic cause.

Possibly the economics textbooks of today are more unrealistic about so-called 'consumer sovereignty' than on any other topic except Marxism. The 'consumers' choice' of capitalism is ritualistically counterposed to the 'state regulation' of socialism almost invariably without any attempt to weigh up the pros and cons of the two systems as they operate in reality. In the real world, consumer choice under capitalism depends on (a) incomes, and these vary enormously, (b) advertising, and no consumer is alive today in the capitalist world who has not to some extent had his choice warped to 'want' what the producer wishes to sell him, and (c) monopoly and near-monopoly, distorting the competitive price system (which kept prices down to 'marginal costs' or near 'values').

In the countries with socialist planning, advertising is limited to what orthodox economists regard as legitimate, i.e. 'informative' advertising only. Price policy is certainly not competitive, since it is planned, and as Marx foresaw, the working population cannot consume until deductions have been made for further development of the economy. While 'profits' are encouraged, these must be made from the lowering of costs through increasing productivity, and the planning of prices ensures their stability, and their reduction in so far as increasing productivity justifies this.

As far as incomes are concerned, no socialist country has a range of incomes comparable with those of capitalist countries where high *unearned* incomes tend to be the largest of all. Estimates vary, but it would seem that differences in earnings in the socialist countries are no greater than differences in *earned* incomes under capitalism, and probably much less.

According to his or her work, the socialist citizen earns a wage. Taxation is far lower than in most capitalist countries on this income, and in the USSR there are no deductions for social insurances—health, unemployment or pensions. As to earnings, there is freedom to spend according to consumers' choice, and the right of 'veto' on goods which are not worth buying. As to the assortment available, this varies from year to year, the general tendency being for a steadily improving, rationally devised, assortment of goods and services as the productivity of society increases.

Today the whole world is thinking in terms of growth and development. Marx, in his day, was already doing this in his study of capitalism, but with full awareness of the in-built contradictions of capitalism which hamper this development, even at the best causing it to take place by fits and starts, booms and slumps, or from 1946 to 1970 in Britain, stop-and-go. Marx was alone in his day in pointing out the vital importance of balance in the economy, between the production of the means of production, and of the means of consumption. He perceived that no lasting balance in this respect was possible because of the nature of capitalism itself.

While problems of growth and development continued to be ignored by the orthodox, the first Marxist State, the USSR, launched out on comprehensive planned growth and development from 1928 onwards, once it had restored the economy to its 1913 level after years of war, revolution and armed intervention. While the USSR grappled with the task of introducing planning in order to catch up with the advanced capitalist world and to reorganise agriculture on co-operative socialist lines, the rest of the world faced the worst economic crisis in its history. This external event had its repercussions on the Soviet Union, since it was obliged to export far more than had been anticipated of its agricultural produce, timber and oil to pay for necessary imports of means of production. The main long-term objectives of the First Five Year Plan were achieved, but the effects on living standards originally anticipated were delayed for yet more years before they were attained.

Despite the rude interruption and destruction of the Second World War, subsequent Five Year Plans have brought the USSR up to the world's second place in production. Successive plans are providing ever rising real incomes, and the current Five Year Plan, adopted in 1971, for the first time provides for consumers' goods to increase in supply more rapidly than means of production.

The peoples of the socialist countries are ready to trade with the capitalist world, and offer a steadily increasing market for other countries' goods. Joint projects are being developed, now even on one territory of developed capitalist countries, as is the case with regard to Soviet co-operation in the building of an iron-and-steel works in France. The development of 'co-operation and competition' between the socialist and capitalist world is regarded by Marxists as an essential feature of 'peaceful coexistence' while opposition to it, even in capitalist countries, is on the decline.

Increasing trade, increasing exchanges of technical know-how, increasing visits in both directions—are all part of peaceful co-existence between two social systems. Exchanges of ideas are taking place, and some of the techniques of orthodox economics, when divested of their capitalism, may prove useful to the countries of planned economy. And some of the ideas of the socialist countries may also be useful to public authorities in the west, so long as they do not impinge too much on the rights of private ownership. But while coexistence and trade are definitely on the agenda, suggestions that the two systems are becoming progressively less distinguishable are misguided, and almost always stem from a refusal to recognise the profound difference between public and private ownership of the means of production.

Just as Marxism and orthodox economics respectively reflect the general outlook appropriate to wage-earners and business-men; even if these outlooks are only consciously adopted by a minority; so the socialist and capitalist countries, 'East' and 'West', are aiming to benefit the working population in the one case, and to further the cause of 'business' in the other, even where a state sector is now accepted.

Within the western countries there is constant conflict between 'bosses and men', 'masters and servants', employers and trade unions; and constant competition, both within and between countries, which involves the largest monopoly concerns them-selves in rivalry with one another. In all capitalist countries there is a striving for a favourable balance of trade ('we must increase our exports'); for limiting wages, sometimes called a 'prices and incomes policy'; for more profit—on the side of the employers; for more wages—on the side of the workers.

In the socialist countries there is also a struggle—for more out-put, for less bureaucracy, and for fulfilling Plans which include the steady improvement of the material and cultural standard of life of the people, for more leisure, and for a further development of the economic system in the future.

This struggle, in the years up to Stalin's death, was greatly distorted in the USSR because an economically backward country was trying to modernise itself, and to raise productivity, in conditions in which large resources had to be set aside for defence. Had it not been for the Five Year Plans started in 1928, the USSR could never have emerged victorious from the trials of 1941–5. Hence, while in theory the aims of immediate material and cultural advance were regarded as equally important with growth and development, in practice the period of the initial accumulation demanded greater sacrifices than would have been necessary in a more harmonious international atmosphere.

The effects of this on subsequent Soviet developments are by no means negligible; but also need not be repeated in other

M

countries in different situations. From the standpoint of Marxism, problems have certainly arisen owing to the fact that the first country to attempt to apply a Marxist solution to the economic problem was a country not of a type most suited to the task as regards its level of economic development. The first working model of 'Marxism in practice' was, in fact, a socialist state which had to carry out on its territory many of the economic tasks which Marx has assumed would be fulfilled by capitalism before it was supplanted. At the same time, the developed capitalist countries which, in Marx's view, were 'ripe' for socialism, are still the scene of the operation of capitalism. These are facts which have come into being since the days of Marx; Marxism has to adapt itself by applying Marx's techniques to the study of these facts.

Orthodox Economics came into existence as a reflection of the English Industrial Revolution. Before industrialisation, there had been forerunners of Political Economy in the Physiocrats and the Mercantilists. But Adam Smith, in his *Wealth of Nations*, founded English Political Economy, renamed Economics by Alfred Marshall at the end of the last century.

Adam Smith and Ricardo laid the foundation on which Marx not uncritically built. Marx was never able to finish the four volumes of *Capital* which he had planned. Vol. III was edited posthumously by Engels, and Vol. IV, *Theories of Surplus Value*, was edited and published in Moscow only after the first Socialist Revolution had taken place.

Both adherents and opponents have often, for their own purposes, one-sidedly selected this or that phrase of Marx in isolation, yet when qualified, as Marx himself qualified it elsewhere, its meaning becomes fuller and in essence quite different. We have given ample examples.

It is to be hoped that, having read this book, any student of orthodox economics will appreciate now that there exists another system of economic thought, based on a different approach, which is worthy of serious study despite the fact that it has been denigrated and misrepresented. Equally, there are two social systems in the world today, and the political economy of the one is no less important than the economics of the other.

In one short book it has not been possible to touch on more than the fringe of a subject which, it is to be hoped, will claim more serious study as time goes on.

How many students of the orthodox Economics of today will become students of Marxist Political Economy tomorrow?—And if they do, let them take care to study what Marx really said and not be misled by pontifical dissertations claiming to explain what Marx 'really' meant!

Postscript

While the present book was already in the press there was published *The Coming Clash*, by Hugh Stephenson, at present editor of the *Times Business News*. The book is such striking confirmation of Marx's and Lenin's view of capitalism as inevitably leading to ever larger and more monopolistic units that it demands quotation here, and is recommended to every reader of the present book.

Supported by ample factual detail Stephenson finds that the interests of present-day 'international corporations increasingly conflict with and disturb the comfortable conventions about the divine rights of the sovereign nation state.' (Op. cit., pp. 7–8.) 'In part, individual governments have already lost their freedom of action' to 'international industry'. (Ibid., p. II.) They are therefore faced with two alternatives: either 'accepting the requirements of international industry' which Marxists would call 'international monopoly capital', or 'following the path of Castro's Cuba.' (Ibid., p. 12.)

It is a pity that Stephenson tends to stress only the *subordination* of states to monopoly capital whereas often nowadays an actual *identification* with monopoly interests takes place. Again, his reference to Cuba could have been supplemented by greater stress on the working-class movement, whatever its present deficiencies, as the only social force capable of rallying opposition to the growing dictatorship of monopolies.

Index